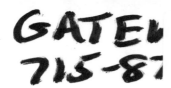

THE ISCH.............

(water color art by Isai Hernandez)

And I saw another mighty angel come down from heaven, clothed with a cloud: and a rainbow was upon his head, and his face was as it were the sun, and his feet as pillars of fire: 2And he had in his hand a little book open: and he set his right foot upon the sea, and his left foot on the earth, 3And cried with a loud voice, as when a lion roareth: and when he had cried, seven thunders uttered their voices. 4And when the seven thunders had uttered their voices, I was about to write: and I heard a voice from heaven saying unto me, Seal up those things which the seven thunders uttered, and write them not. 5And the angel which I saw stand upon the sea and upon the earth lifted up his hand to heaven, 6And sware by him that liveth for ever and ever, who created heaven, and the things that therein are, and the earth, and the things that therein are, and the sea, and the things which are therein, that there should be time no longer: 7But in the days of the voice of the seventh angel, when he shall begin to sound, the mystery of God should be finished, as he hath declared to his servants the prophets. 8And the voice which I heard from heaven spake unto me again, and said, Go and take the little book which is open in the hand of the angel which standeth upon the sea and upon the earth. 9And I went unto the angel, and said unto him, Give me the little book. And he said unto me, Take it, and eat it up; and it shall make thy belly bitter, but it shall be in thy mouth sweet as honey. 10And I took the little book out of the angel's hand, and ate it up; and it was in my mouth sweet as honey: and as soon as I had eaten it, my belly was bitter. 11And he said unto me, Thou must prophesy again before many peoples, and nations, and tongues, and kings.

Revelations 10:1-11

GATEWOODS
715-877-2413

SEERS

catalog

by Ron Crawford

PNEUMATIKOS PUBLISHING
P.O. 595351
Dallas, TX 75359
www.pneumatikos.com
info@pneumatikos.com

© 2002 by Ron Crawford

Published by Pneumatikos Publishing
P.O. Box 593531
Dallas, TX 75359
E-Mail: info@pneumatikos.com
www.pneumatikos.com

First printing, September, 2002
Second printing, January, 2003
Third printing, September, 2003

ISBN #0-9720681-4-7

Cover Art Work by Fabian Arroyo
Illustrations by Isai Hernandez

Unless otherwise noted, scripture quotations are from the HOLY BIBLE, Authorized King James Version.

Printed in the United States by Morris Publishing
3212 East Highway 30
Kearney, NE 68847
1-800-650-7888

table of contents

preface

There is a fictitious story told from the pages of the Old West that bears remarkable insights concerning the church of today. The story goes something like this.

Two cowboys were riding along a desolate roadway when they came upon a Native American scout. He was laying crosswise on the trail with his entire body stretched flatly upon the ground. Immediately, the approaching cowboys dismounted from their horses and rushed to the aid of the Indian.

The travelers knelt down alongside the prostrated man and inquired as to what he was doing. In response to their question, the scout uttered these words: "Two stagecoach, each pulled by four horses; three outlaws on fast moving horses chasing stagecoach; two dogs; one buzzard."

To this detailed report, the cowboys reacted in absolute amazement. One looked at the other and said, "Isn't it incredible that this scout can lay his ear to the ground and tell us what is coming up the road?" The Indian painfully replied, "That not coming! It run over me yesterday!"

What a picture of the modern church! Our Seers are accurate in proclaiming tragedies that have already occurred. We are wonderful at detailing that which has already transpired. The contemporary watchman is good at numbering; but lousy at providing precise warning. The friends of God are not close enough to Him to proclaim what He is about to do. Our leadership is more interested in preserving that which has passed than moving into the fresh things that God desires for His church and planet. The trumpet gives a polished but uncertain sound. Few mobilize in response.

These observations are closely aligned with the days of young Samuel. The eyes of the church are dim, and there is little open vision. No wonder the people of God are more inclined to fear the future rather than proclaim it, trusting in a rapture that will remove them from an uncertain horizon.

EXHORTATION FROM THE BOOK OF REVELATION

Jesus spoke powerful words to His seven churches in the beginning chapters of the Book of Revelation. Although He offered direct insights to each individual church, He reiterated one thing to all of them. This singular insight is the watchword of His heart to the church today: "He that hath an ear, let him hear what the Spirit saith to the churches."

This injunction is a current *rhema* to the Body of Christ. We must become proficient at knowing our God and what He would speak to us. We must not be reliant upon the delinquent analysis of immobile establishment. Our need is for a current and strategic word for today and tomorrow. This is what God is offering, as it is an absolute necessity for survival and victory in our lives in the present day.

WHY A SEERS CATALOG?

This writing is not intended to be an encyclopedia of all things spiritual. In fact, it is basically intended to stir you into a mode of inquiry and acquisition. The name has been chosen to typify and capture a thought process that should be familiar to just about everyone.

When I was a little boy, I loved to look through catalogs from retail stores. On each page I saw things that I knew would bring absolute fulfillment to my life. My imagination would capture each item for sale, and I could envision exactly how I would enjoy each one. Especially before Christmas and Birthday, these catalogs were well worn by the perusal of my fingers and eyes. I wanted everything! Although my family was not financially able to afford the things that I beheld, the fun of seeing and desiring opened my thoughts into a world much larger than that which I previously had known.

The beauty of this catalog is that your Heavenly Father offers powerful giftings to all who will come to Him. These gifts are not meant to titillate or entertain. Rather, they are spiritual things that we need and that God desperately desires for us to appropriate into our lives. This catalog is one of relationship and service to our Heavenly Father.

What things listed here has God already given and what does He desire for you to acquire? God stands ready to open His storehouse for you as He desires to give good gifts to His children. He longs to pour out His Spirit upon His sons and daughters, offering to each person exactly that which is needed to find happiness, fulfillment and triumph. Are you willing to pay the necessary price of devotion and faith?

WHO SHOULD READ THIS BOOK?

There are many that would attribute foolishness to the statements made herein due to simple unbelief. Others, deeming themselves the bastion of all things spiritual, will promote prohibition of such discussions due to a control or pharisaic spirit. There is very little that can be done in regard to these opinions, other than to ignore such protestation. Jesus took this approach in response to the naysayer that frequented His ministry.

Milton stated, "I write for the fit audience, though few." He inferred that the common man was incapable of grasping his work. May God grant to us a large spirit and an open mind to receive the uncommon that He freely offers. Many are called, but few are chosen.

There are many people that have sensory giftings that are supernatural in nature. It is vital that these gifts be developed and placed into their proper order according to the purpose of Almighty God. If you are reading this book and you have not been born again into the Kingdom of God through the acceptance of Jesus Christ, you must do this immediately. Ask God to forgive your sins, cleansing them by the blood of Jesus. Devote your life to Him and align yourself immediately in a Bible-believing, Spirit-filled congregation.

If you are a Seer, you must have two things that are continually operative in your life. First, you must be a student of the Bible as it is the basis upon which all things are judged. It will serve as your direction through many peculiar pathways. Various areas of the spirit realm are deceptive and confusing even for the most experienced servant of God. Hiding the Word in your heart will help you avoid the sin that could cause you to miss the mark.

The second imperative for the Seer is to be an intercessor. You do not have to be an intercessor in order to see; but to be a true and effective Seer, you must be close to the heart of God. This can only come through time spent with Him. Without His passion, there is no real purpose for your gift or life. A Seer without purpose and accountability is a free agent in the spirit realm, and that is a dangerous and risky business.

An additional element in favor of the process of intercession is that praying in tongues is the speaking of mysteries. The more you commune with God in this manner, the more you will discuss mysteries with God. Interpreting these mysteries is the privilege of a Seer.

Admittedly, not everyone is a Seer. Regardless of your particular gifting within the Body of Christ, it is imperative that the army of God recognize this important endowment. Without radar, surveillance, and proper knowledge of the terrain ahead, a modern army is basically useless.

During the American Civil War, the Battle of Gettysburg was arguably the telling conflict of the entire war. The armies of North and South faced off against each other on the farm fields of south central Pennsylvania in a battle that would determine the course of North America. The gallant and brilliant General Robert E. Lee was at the helm of the Southern army. All of his experience, charisma and daring could not provide what was needed for victory in that battle. He desperately needed one necessary weapon that was precariously missing, his eyes. In the eighteenth century, the Seer of the army was the cavalry. At Gettysburg, J.E.B. Stuart and Lee's cavalry were delinquent in arriving at the battle. Due to this lack of insight, Lee was unable to employ the things that made him a victorious commander. Subsequently, the battle was lost, and the South never recovered the opportunity to win the War. The church must have eyes that are firmly fixed upon the things that God is doing today. Without the Seer's vision, the people will perish.

May our ears hear and our eyes see.

seers introduction

Are you amazed by the preponderance of available information regarding the spirit realm? It is absolutely phenomenal to witness the manner in which television, film and the printed media have become a training ground for the things of the dark realm. Visiting a local bookstore or watching the previews of upcoming films can regularly be considered nothing other than a blatant recruitment technique for the enemy.

These are incredible days of spiritual acuity and perception. Television and film seem to be concentrating on the sphere of insight into the spirit realm. The scheduling of broadcast medium has been populated with diverse programming concerning psychic phenomenon, necromancy, witchcraft, occultic warfare and many other vile forms of propaganda from the dark realm. Hollywood continues to produce films that indoctrinate the culture with evil in all its forms, and we are being systematically de-sensitized to evil. Like the frog in an increasingly boiling kettle of water, we do not really know the depth of our desperation.

Our children see the depiction of demonic beings within the "cartoons" that are daily shown on the small screen. Upon a recent perusal of one of these "harmless" offerings, I heard the names of two ruling demons, endured the reading of a dark incantation and listened as a character explained the connection between the two. Some of the most prominent children's films of the past few years have been nothing short of basic training for witchcraft.

Bookstores are a spawning ground for occultist material. Innocent people are unknowing accomplices of the doctrines of demons. Eastern religions have infiltrated the decorating industry, and the most fashionable homes in town are color coordinated to match chakra with desire in a white witchcraft genre. The signs of the New Age and of the unveiling of spiritual information are not only all around us but are drenching the soil of our terrain.

The tragedy of all of this is that the enemy is utilizing the ways of God to his own advantage, twisting these powerful truths into corrupted tools of domination. Satan and his fallen comrades were well schooled in the ways of God before the rebellion against God. The Bible speaks of Satan in the person of the king of Tyre as being able to "seal up the sum." This simply means that he knows how things are to be done. The verse continues by saying that he does this wisely in order to manifest a beautiful appearance.

> Ezekiel 28:12   Son of man, take up a lamentation upon the king of Tyrus, and say unto him, Thus saith the Lord God; Thou sealest up the sum, full of wisdom, and perfect in beauty.

A chief lieutenant of the enemy is a being named Behemoth, and he is depicted as being the chief of the ways of God. The cited passage from Job says that this being is so powerful that God would only send a Cherub-level angel to deal with him. The operative understanding is that the ways of God are paramount to the success of the enemy kingdom.

> Job 40:19   He is the *chief* of *the ways* of God: he that made him can make his sword (*cherub*) to approach unto him.

The enemy asserted his grasp of the ways of God in the passage that speaks most powerfully of the demise of Satan. Isaiah declares that the enemy was so convinced of the power of the ways of God that he felt his understanding of them could overcome God Himself. This knowledgeable assumption speaks volumes concerning the power of the ways of God. It also tells us that the enemy intends to employ the application of these ways in order to empower and administer his evil kingdom.

> Isaiah 14:14   I will ascend above the heights of the clouds; I will be like the most High.

It is high time for the children of God to put on the armor of light, or the ways of God. We must awaken to the evil influences that have subtly and blatantly infiltrated our world.

> Romans 13:11-12   And that, knowing the time, that now it is high time to awake out of sleep: for now is our salvation nearer than when we believed. [12] The night is far spent, the day is at hand: let us therefore cast off the works of darkness, and let us put on the armour of light.

For the most part, the church has been ignorant of the potent manner in which the Kingdom of God operates. We have chosen to abide in a general state of existence and have left much of the territory of the spirit realm to the agents of darkness. Consequently, the works of the righteousness of God are not being regularly accomplished by His people. Jesus spoke of this in the Gospel of Luke.

> Luke 16:8   And the lord commended the unjust steward, because he had done wisely: for the children of this world are in their generation wiser than the children of light.

An unjust servant is literally a servant who has not accomplished the righteousness or purposes of his Lord. Emulating this pursuit, the church utilizes the power at their disposal in order to cater to themselves and their own needs. God tells us that if we initially seek His Kingdom and righteousness that God will take care of our needs. The unjust servant was commended when he finally began the process of reaping a return on that which belonged to his master.

Jesus continues the teaching in Luke 16 by advising the believer to become familiar with the ways of those who deal in earthly wealth. Ideally, these worldly fortune builders employ spiritual principles to amass their capital. Recently, I read an article in a leading business journal that discussed the style in which successful business ventures begin. Reputation and livelihood must be staked upon uncharted territory. Something new has no track record and subsequently is felt to be wrong from the outset by just about everybody in the know. Everyone, that is, except for the visionary that sees the possibilities and understands the timing.

The resurrected Jesus told a doubtful Thomas that people would be blessed when they did not insist on seeing with a tangible eye before believing. Paul writes in 2 Corinthians 4:18 that the eye of the spiritual must supercede the eye of the temporal.

The ways of God belong to us as His children, and His winds can readily be discerned by those that seek Him. At times, God will grant a grace gift in order to allow someone to be able to discern these winds in extraordinary measure. The enemy has duped us into thinking that the gift of discerning of spirits is solely for the purpose of knowing what is demonic and what is not.

Experts in the business of detecting counterfeit bills are trained by knowing the characteristic feel of legitimate currency, and God is no different in His training technique. As we discern and learn His ways, we are able to conduct His business and detect the presence of the enemy with great clarity. There is a group of people known as the *Pneumatikos* in the New Testament, and they are literally the wind people. These influential individuals are said to understand the ways of God and are destined to supervise the implementation of these ways within and through the church.

The Seer is needed in order to gain the vision of God for these last days. To see God and to know His ways is the apex of existence for the church. It has been well said that all that is necessary for evil to prevail is for good men and women to do nothing. It is high time to learn how to become the Children of Light and to be wiser than the children of the world.

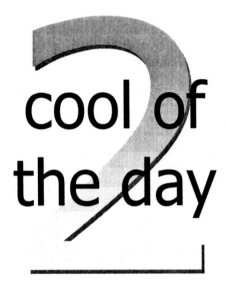

**cool of
the day**

Why did God create mankind? Simple enough question, isn't it?

Traditional religious commentary regarding this question will generally depict God as being some type of lonely individual in need of a measure of companionship. Although God delights in fellowship with us, He did not create Adam and Eve to be His "little buddies." God created mankind to partner with Him and to do His bidding upon this planet.

The bidding of God remains the same as it has been since the creation of mankind. God has had a desire for man and woman to be His agents upon the earth. In the first chapter of Genesis, God told Adam that he was going to be entrusted with five responsibilities and privileges.

> Genesis 1:28   And God blessed them, and God said unto them, Be fruitful, and multiply, and replenish the earth, and subdue it: and have dominion over the fish of the sea, and over the fowl of the air, and over every living thing that moveth upon the earth.

Note that God commissioned man to accomplish five things upon the earth. Without taking liberties with interpretation, it is quite simple to align these five things with the five-fold giftings of the New Testament.

1. Fruitfulness – *Parah*

Fruitfulness can be aligned with the Office of the Prophet. Jesus told us in John 15 that if we abide in Him, we will produce much fruit. Without Him, we can do nothing.

> **John 15:5**   I am the vine, ye are the branches: He that abideth in me, and I in him, the same bringeth forth much fruit: for without me ye can do nothing.

This theme of fruitfulness is again detailed in Amos. God says that He will reveal His secret or intimate things to His Prophets. The Prophet knows the heart of God through commune with Him, and the Prophet aligns with this commission to bear much fruit.

> **Amos 3:7**   Surely the Lord God will do nothing, but he revealeth his secret unto his servants the prophets.

Fruitfulness comes from closeness with God, and the Word says that God will not do anything unless He first shares it with His dearest companions in the form of precious secrets.

2. Multiplying – *Rabah*

Multiplying means "to define, elaborate and properly utilize." Understanding what is being provided and fully utilizing it is crucial to doing the work of God. The task of multiplying corresponds to the Office of Teacher, which also correlates with the Office of the Seer. This is further detailed in Chapter 8.

3. Replenishing – *Mala*

"To replenish" can also be translated as "to complete, to be a messenger, to accomplish or fulfill." Following after the Prophet and Teacher, this word can only correspond to the Office of the Apostle. Take special note that this commandment applies to the earth.

4. Subduing – *Kabash*

Have you ever heard of someone "putting the kabash" on someone or something? Literally, that means that a conquering has occurred. To subdue is to take charge, to domineer, to supercede in a specific manner or way. This applies to the Office of the Evangelist as the miracle power of the Lord is visited upon a place or thing.

5. Dominating – *Radah*

To have dominion means to rule and reign wisely. This easily corresponds to the Office of the Pastor.

God is consistent with all that He does. What He originally intended for mankind on this planet is what He still intends. The five-fold giftings apply to the earth and to all that dwell therein and upon.

THE EARTH AND THE PEOPLE

The earth had originally been created as a masterpiece of worship. Genesis 1:1 tells us that in the very beginning, God created the heaven and the earth. Since God does all things well, this creation was magnificent. From the revelation of the Scriptures, we recognize that every part of creation can give glory and praise to the Lord God.

Something happened between the first and second verses of Genesis 1. The wondrous creation of Verse 1 becomes the formless and void site of Verse 2. The term "without form and void" was an ancient colloquialism that described the aftermath of a climactic battle. In the book of Jeremiah, we see this picture in fuller detail.

> Jeremiah 4:23   I beheld the earth, and, lo, it was without form, and void; and the heavens, and they had no light.

Undoubtedly, the disastrous gap was caused by the rebellion of Satan, and the destruction that ensued. This cataclysmic event wreaked havoc upon the beauties of the earth and effectively suspended much of the purposes constructed within.

The Bible says in Genesis 1:2 that the wind, *ruach,* of God moved upon the face of the waters of this void. God created man so that the earth, which belongs to Him, might be redeemed. By this, God intended to restore the original purposes and usages of the earth. Man was to partner with God in this great pursuit. In doing so, many of the tasks and duties of the fallen ones would now be attended by mankind in conjunction with the holy angels.

Ancient places would now be resurrected and redeemed for their original function of worshipping and serving God. The Most High would gradually train and equip man for these purposes. The Tree of the Knowledge of Good and Evil was a depiction and source of the *towb*, or good purpose of God, and the *ra*, or evil twisting and perversion of the enemy. Adam and Eve were not to access this tree at their own discretion. The knowledge that was contained within this tree was to be defined by the mouth of God to His children. Only then could the process of obedience and authority be applied within the wisdom of the Lord.

WALKING WITH GOD

A unique picture of this fellowship and training is found in the verse that forms the title of this chapter.

> Genesis 3:8   And they heard the voice of the Lord God walking in the garden in the cool of the day: and Adam and his wife hid themselves from the presence of the Lord God amongst the trees of the garden.

During a Texas summer, the best time to be outdoors is in the early morning or early evening. The temperatures are much more pleasant during those "cooler" times of the day. Many assume that this verse speaks of an hour during the Edenic day that was more preferable than any other. We must recognize that in Eden, there was no such necessity, as there was perfect climate at all times.

Quite literally, the cool of the day means the *ruach* of the day. It was the time that God would come into the garden to commune with Adam and Eve. This is the second appearance of the word *ruach* in the Bible; the first being when the Spirit of God moved, or brooded, upon the face of the shapeless deep.

The Genesis account tells us that the voice of God came through His wind. Extrapolating from this theme, we can easily deduce that in order to hear clearly from God, we must fellowship within His winds to properly ascertain and implement His purpose. God loves to share His plans with those to whom He has begun the process of partnership.

God's Spirit will always attend to that which belongs to Him. This *ruach,* or wind, is the expression of His person and ways. It is through the manifestation of His Seven Spirits that He depicts the progression of how He does things. While we will further explore this truth within the next chapter, it is important for this discussion that we recognize the training of Adam and Eve in the purposes and ways of God. There was nothing further to create upon the earth or within the heaven, so the topic of revelation must have focused upon the redemption of the original footstool of God. This discussion would have entailed the places of worship with corresponding anointings that are strategically positioned throughout the planet.

The fallen angels had once been attendants of the worship of God at these sites. Realistically, they still are encamped about the places of their former duty and service to God. Since the schooling of Adam and Eve meant the demise of the remaining vestiges of enemy encampment, it was critical from a satanic standpoint that Adam rebel and that the purpose of God not be detailed. This was the objective of the serpent, and it was successful.

We find God coming to commune with Adam and Eve in the same manner He had done for an unspecified number of days. After the disobedience, Adam and Eve hid within the trees that symbolized the former service to God. They covered themselves with leaves of the fig tree, symbolic of the fruits of happiness and commune.

These fallen humans strove to recapture the thrill of a victory from yesterday. They were told that they were naked and became ashamed. Simply put, they should not have been embarrassed around each other. There were no neighbors to avoid. Being ashamed and naked had to be indicative of their lack of confidence that God could use them further.

Often, the enemy will tell the believer that God cannot be trusted in grand ways, and that they should abide in the shadow of former victory. After all, enjoy the fruits of yesterday and do not risk anything. Do not attempt anything crucial or innovative for God might let you down. This is the abiding fruit of the Tree of Good and Evil. The objective of the enemy remains the same: do not flow in the Winds of the Spirit and do not fulfill God's mandate for the planet.

INIQUITIES AND THE COMMONPLACE

Most people fail to be attuned to the spirit realm around them because of two reasons. The first is endemic with Adam's fall, and that is the base of iniquity within the individual life. The second is a pre-occupation with the commonplace or ordinary. Let us briefly look at the hindrance of iniquity as it is revealed through the life of Jacob.

The name Jacob literally means "supplanter," and it was given him by reason of the manner in which he and his twin brother, Esau, were born. When Jacob grabbed the heel of his sibling during the birthing process, it showed a measure of character within him that would follow him for the rest of his life. He utilized his devious mannerisms in order to gain the family birthright; and although God attempted to change his name to Israel, meaning "God strives," Jacob continued to be Jacob throughout the rest of his earthly existence.

Anyone that will be a person of destiny must be open to the realm of God's Spirit. The hand of God was continually manifested in the life of Jacob, but Jacob was often too encumbered with his own ways to realize this blessing. Once, Jacob found himself in a place called Mahanaim, or the double camp (Genesis 32:2). This was a place where the host, or army of God's angels was present. Instead of trusting in the provision of the spirit realm, Jacob relied upon his own cunning and deceitful nature to prepare for an encounter with his brother Esau.

On another occasion, Jacob experienced the mighty presence of God at Bethel (Genesis 20:16). Even though he witnessed the transport of angels proceeding back and forth between the earth and the heavens, he did not recognize the fact that God was there. He said that God was in the place, but he knew it not, and this phrase could be echoed throughout much of the history of mankind. We are simply too involved with our own ways to entertain God.

If iniquity does not encumber us, the commonplace might just keep us from seeing and experiencing the presence of the Lord. This fact is demonstrated in the passage which speaks of the burning bush in Exodus 3:1-4. Moses had walked this very ground any number of times while conducting his business of tending the flocks. Mt. Horeb has always been a place of terrific spiritual sensitivity, and we see this by virtue of the many illustrations throughout the Bible. Moses had undoubtedly witnessed hints of the manifestation of God's presence throughout the months of his sojourning. When he turned from his own pathway to see God, God met him because of his choice to pursue the Most High.

God is still in the business of revealing the purposes of this planet to His Saints; however, this is a meticulous process and must be achieved in accordance with the exact timetable of God. Those who will turn aside from their own pathways and shortcomings in order to devote themselves to God and His ways will find Him. The Almighty still utters His voice from the midst of His winds. His purposes are still depicted in His stated progression of covenant.

PEOPLE AND THE PLANET

When Adam sinned, God implemented a plan through which He would redeem the people as well as the planet. Throughout the lives of the patriarchs, God was developing a people that would follow Him in fulfilling His original intent for Adam and the earth. This is what Jesus came to accomplish as He redeemed man to God in order to reveal the purposes of the Father upon and within His entire creation.

The Christian community mistakenly believes that God solely wants to redeem people. For the most part, these folk do not view God as being overly concerned about the earth itself. We must look carefully at the Bible to ascertain the truth.

John 3:16   For God so loved the world, that he gave his only begotten Son, that whosoever believeth in him should not perish, but have everlasting life.

Psalm 24:1   The earth is the Lord's, and the fulness thereof; the world, and they that dwell therein.

Psalm 98:7   Let the sea roar, and the fulness thereof; the world, and they that dwell therein.

Psalm 98:9   Before the Lord; for he cometh to judge the earth: with righteousness shall he judge the world, and the people with equity.

Mark 16:15   And he said unto them, Go ye into all the world, and preach the gospel to every creature.

1 Corinthians 4:9   For I think that God hath set forth us the apostles last, as it were appointed to death: for we are made a spectacle unto the world, and to angels, and to men.

God desires His people to know that He is very much interested in them and the planet on which they dwell. His winds still move upon His creation. In order to be the people that God can use in this day, we must discern His winds and flow with them. Our hearts must be devoted to Him and His purposes, and we must flee inherent iniquity and our own agendas in order to see and fellowship with the Most High.

seven spirits of God and God's covenant

As post–Adamic mankind progressed upon the face of the earth, it became increasingly apparent that the adversary was intent upon destroying the plan of God for humanity. In the days of Noah, the Bible tells us that man's imagination was continually evil.

> Genesis 6:5   And God saw that the wickedness of man was great in the earth, and that every imagination of the thoughts of his heart was only evil continually.

When Adam ate of the Tree of the Knowledge of Good and Evil, he did much more than disobey God's edict of abstinence. This tree held both evil (*ra*) and good (*towb*). Literally, the fruit was God's expression of the difference between His perfect purpose and the twisting of that purpose through rebellion and pride.

It is my feeling that God wanted to progressively teach Adam and Eve the difference between these two elements. Evil will always go indiscriminately beyond and ahead of the timetable of God. Those that follow God into the deeper things need not fear falling behind, but going too far ahead of God's timing. This was the case with Adam, and the enemy knew it.

To the offspring of Adam, in the day of Noah the imagination of the thoughts of the heart was continually *ra*, or evil. Additionally, the women of the earth began to intermingle with demonic influences, and the fabric of the creation of man was at stake. God stated in response that His Spirit, or *ruach*, would not continue to strive with man. Further, the Bible says that the time of the end would be as it was in the days of Noah. Specifically, this has much to do with good and evil, and to which man will turn.

The eyes of the Lord found Noah. Subsequently, grace was apportioned to him, and he was delivered from destruction. In order to glean what this means to us, we must explore the meaning of God's eyes, His spirits and His covenant for the planet.

THE EYES OF THE LORD

> Genesis 6:8   But Noah found grace in the eyes of the Lord.

> Revelation 1:4   John to the seven churches which are in Asia: Grace be unto you, and peace, from him which is, and which was, and which is to come; and from the seven Spirits which are before his throne;

Grace is a magnificent commodity. It is this aspect of God's nature that causes mankind to gain help in transitioning from one level to another. We correctly associate grace with the transaction of becoming born again. Grace does not cease at salvation. The New Testament tells us that believers ought to grow in grace, and that the early church enjoyed great grace. Plainly spoken, grace will always be present when God does a work of deliverance or promotion.

Wherever the eyes of the Lord are found, grace will be there. The Bible says that the eyes of the Lord go forth throughout the entire earth, to exhibit exploits on behalf of those who will walk in humility according to His purposes. He is more interested in character and devotion than skill or appearance.

> 2 Chronicles 16:9   For the eyes of the Lord run to and fro throughout the whole earth, to shew himself strong in the behalf of them whose heart is perfect toward him. Herein thou hast done foolishly: therefore from henceforth thou shalt have wars.

God does not look for the most likely before He invests His fantastic power. He seems to delight in the least likely candidate or most desperate situation. This was the case with Zerubbabel in the Book of Zechariah.

> Zechariah 4:10   For who hath despised the day of small things? for they shall rejoice, and shall see the plummet in the hand of Zerubbabel with those seven; they are the eyes of the Lord, which run to and fro through the whole earth.

The eyes of the Lord that were seen upon the cornerstone in Zechariah 4 are synonymous with the Seven Spirits of God. In Revelation we find a clear association between the seven eyes and the Seven Spirits of God.

> Revelation 5:6   And I beheld, and, lo, in the midst of the throne and of the four beasts, and in the midst of the elders, stood a Lamb as it had

been slain, having seven horns and seven eyes,
which are the seven Spirits of God sent forth into
all the earth.

Trinitarians rightly assert that our God is Triune in personality, fully displaying Himself as Father, Son and Holy Spirit. We do not often discuss the facet of God which displays Seven Spirits, but these are very much a part of His character and purpose. God's Seven Spirits are addressed in the writing to the church at Sardis.

Revelation 3:1   And unto the angel of the
church in Sardis write; These things saith he that
hath the seven Spirits of God, and the seven
stars; I know thy works, that thou hast a name
that thou livest, and art dead.

Jesus identifies the seven stars within His right hand as being the angels of the churches (Revelation 1:20). Prophetically, these angels move among, and on behalf of, the churches. The Seven Spirits will look throughout the earth for willing people and churches. Jesus said in Matthew 18:20 that if two or three gather according to the purpose of His name, He would be in the very center of them. He comes to those that are dedicated to His service.

This was the case with Noah, and God's eyes found him.

THE BOW OF COVENANT

After the flood had abated from the face of Mt. Ararat, God spoke to Noah and made a covenantal agreement with him concerning the earth. God placed His rainbow in the sky as a covenant between mankind and Himself.

> Genesis 9:13, 17   I do set my bow in the cloud, and it shall be for a token of a covenant between me and the earth.: [17] And God said unto Noah, This is the token of the covenant, which I have established between me and all flesh that is upon the earth.

The rainbow is God's signature of covenant for the earth. It consists of seven colors and has not altered in appearance or variation of pattern since the first day that Noah witnessed it in the sky. There is much significance to these seven colors and their revealed pattern.

In many ways, the enemy has tried to steal the power and symbolism of this signature of God. The rainbow has become a trademark symbol of some of the most perverted and demonically driven organizations that civilization has known. In most instances the rainbow is shown as having only six colors. Conveniently, the enemy eliminates the one color that most typifies God's glory.

Nobody can remove the full display of God's signature from the sky. Whenever it is revealed through the prism of light and water, the full seven colors of the Lord's pattern are witnessed. Within them, we readily behold the pattern of how God's purpose manifests itself. Each of the colors is a showcase of one of the Seven Spirits of God.

For Noah, God was offering a partnership of extreme proportion. Here was a man that had been delivered from certain destruction. He was also a man that now had the entire world at his disposal. God was with him in covenant and companionship. Sadly, Noah did not realize his blessing, and the purposes of God were not fully realized in his life.

The rainbow still shines in our sky. We have the opportunity to partner with God to accomplish all that He wants to do on the earth. The Seven Spirits still look for a person that will apply for the privilege of serving God in unfathomable dimension.

THE SEVEN LAMPS

God reiterates His offer to the church of the last days through another sign of His Seven Spirits, the lamp.

> Revelation 4:5   And out of the throne proceeded lightnings and thunderings and voices: and there were seven lamps of fire burning before the throne, which are the seven Spirits of God.

In this powerful passage, the Seven Spirits of God are described as lamps. The lamp is an incredible theme found throughout the pages of the Bible, providing light in a very intimate manner for the child of God, and depicting the closeness of God to His people.

It is appropriate that the lamp was a prominent part of God's covenant appearance to Abraham in Genesis 15. Abraham was the father of all who walk in faith, and it was through this encounter that righteousness was first depicted to mankind. God called Abraham "righteous" simply for believing things that were seen with the eye of his spirit.

> Genesis 15:17-18   And it came to pass, that, when the sun went down, and it was dark, behold a smoking furnace, and a burning lamp that passed between those pieces. [18] In the same day the Lord made a covenant with Abram, saying, Unto thy seed have I given this land, from the river of Egypt unto the great river, the river Euphrates:

God desires to invest covenant relationship with people. Since the rebellion of Satan, it has always been God's intent to share the earth with man and to reveal His ways in the process. Whether it be Noah, Abraham or the church of the last days, God wants to reveal His mysteries to a people that will believe in Him and partner with Him. These mysteries will point the way to a partnership with God's Seven Spirits. As it is with the Tribe of Issachar, the Seer will be integral in discerning the seasons of God and knowing what the people of God should do during those seasons.

One of the most intriguing usages of the lamp in the New Testament is found in the parable of the ten virgins. The operative understanding is that which compares union with God and the operation of lamps.

> Matthew 25:1-4   Then shall the kingdom of heaven be likened unto ten virgins, which took their lamps, and went forth to meet the bridegroom. [2] And five of them were wise, and

> five were foolish. [3] They that were foolish took
> their lamps, and took no oil with them: [4] But
> the wise took oil in their vessels with their lamps.

The five wise virgins were prepared to do the bidding of God. The adroit handling of their lamps indicated that they were desirous of them being able to burn and operate efficiently. Their lamps were filled with oil, indicating a communing partnership with God.

The five foolish virgins were more interested in convenience, relying on others for the relational insights that God freely grants to those who love Him. The Greek word for foolish is *moros*, a derivative of *musterion*. *Musterion* is that dimension of mystery that continuously reveals clues and juncture points regarding the overall purpose of God. Literally, these foolish ones were unprepared by virtue of their lack of attention to the signs around them and a decided inattentiveness to the ways of God.

In the following chapters, we will discover the progression of God's purposes as revealed in the unveiling of the identity of His Seven Spirits. For the purposes of this chapter, the message of God is clear. Whoever will come before Him in sincerity and devotion will be a ready candidate for the privilege of partnering with the Most High at His footstool.

the colors
of
the wind

For many, the concept of the Seven Spirits of God is vague and perhaps intimidating. Significant portions of the church world have difficulty indoctrinating the concept of the Holy Spirit Himself, let alone the dimension of seven through which He reveals Himself.

Almighty God has shown Himself in very tangible ways throughout the course of time. Notably, the first two members of the Trinity have been prominently depicted to man. God the Father revealed Himself to Moses and showed His person to Elijah. His voice was heard on many significant occasions by personages within the Scripture. Jesus came as the embodiment of God's Son in order that we might know Him in a physical manner.

The personification of the Holy Spirit has been somewhat elusive. God's Word declares that the Spirit was the active force upon the face of the globe in Genesis 1. It was the Spirit of God that brought life to Adam. For Zechariah, the Spirit took precedence over might and power. God's Spirit breathed life into a fledgling church on the Day of Pentecost. Literally, God's Spirit is the impetus of existence. When Jesus ascended to the Father, the Holy Spirit was sent to become the active presence of God upon the earth.

Holy Spirit literally means "saintly wind." In these days, God is raising up a group of people that will demonstrate the fullness of the Spirit. The Saints of God will be the vessels of the Seven Spirits of the Lord, demonstrating His ways by fulfilling His purposes within the framework of His timing. There will be no limit to what God can do through them, for they will embody and model the very purpose of God.

Each of the Seven Spirits of God are defined by colors. The perception and understanding of these colors can help identify what anointing is present and what God is doing at a particular time. Colors can identify the predominant gifting of an individual. Interpreting color patterns in a scene or situation can help the believer to know what is coming next according to God's pattern. If a sequence is established but a connecting color is missing, this can be an indication of an area wherein God desires to concentrate intercession and refinement.

Understanding the meaning of the colors of the Seven Spirits of God can help us in our interpretation of many vignettes in the Word of God. For instance, reading about the stated colors of an angel in a description found in the Bible can help us interpret that passage in ways that have been heretofore unknown. When we read in Revelation about a color that surrounds the Throne, we can further grasp the intent of God at that moment.

HOW THE DEFINITIONS CAME

When God began to instruct me concerning the importance of color, He did it in a most unusual manner. As I would minister to someone, I could often see a predominant color surrounding or upon them. After the particular session of ministry, I would note what I had seen.

Patterns began to emerge that identified certain colors with particular manifestations of ministry. I would often associate particular colors with ministry giftings that I knew to be present in the individual. Through the course of time, noticeable patterns developed that provided definition to that which God was revealing about Himself.

Whatever we do must be rooted and grounded in the Scripture. Finding Seven Spirits in the Bible was not a problem at all. In fact, there seemed to be no shortage of references to this or that spirit. Through much prayer and study, a concise grouping of the verses that referred to certain Spirits emerged into seven distinct categories. These seven were aligned with the revealed progression of colors. Hence, the color chart that has been provided for you in this catalog.

I would not be so bold as to affix any measure of infallibility to these associations of color and meaning. However, they have borne themselves to be reliable in precept and application. The point is that this is an interpretation of the things that are found in the Bible. The concept of interpreting the Word of God is nothing new as it can be amply located within any Christian bookstore in your local community. Associating color with His Spirit is relatively unknown. I can only attest to the sincerity of my heart in this matter as well as the proof of ministry within and through my local church.

HOW COLOR IS REVEALED IN THE RAINBOW

Those that study light and color will attest to the fact that the spectrum of the rainbow is dependent upon the magnitude of light energy that is able to penetrate through the prism. A stronger factor of light is necessary to witness all seven colors in the sky, while a weaker power factor will only allow for several colors on the scale of seven.

If the rainbow were a meter, red would be the easiest color to depict. The energy waves of red appear in a large and unhurried pattern. At the other end of the spectrum is violet, requiring the highest volume of light energy in order to be seen. The energy waves of violet are quick, concise and condensed. Regardless of the intensity of light, the sequential progression of the colors in the rainbow remains the same and does not vary at all in succession.

This is God's signature, and it reveals His ways and purpose for the earth. Within this chapter, we will specifically address the seven colors of the rainbow in accordance with the representative Spirits of God. The following will serve as our flow chart as we study the magnificent ways of our God.

The colors of the rainbow reveal the progression of how God deals with us as sons, and how we deal with His purposes as sons. Wonderfully, the progression of colors also aligns perfectly with the teaching of Jesus in the Sermon on the Mount. The color pattern detailed in the rainbow is the blueprint that God chose, and we will not attempt to improve upon the perfect.

SPIRITS OF GOD

Revelation 1:4
John to the seven churches which are in Asia: Grace be unto you, and peace, from him which is, and which was, and which is to come; and from the seven Spirits which are before his throne;

COLOR OF RAINBOW	SPIRIT OF GOD	SCRIPTURE REFERENCE	APPLICATION	NAMES OF GOD	ARMOR OF LIGHT	OPPOSING DEMONIC ENTITY	CHARACTERISTIC SPIRITS
Red	Judgment & Burning	Isaiah 4:4 Isaiah 28:6	Alignment with God's Purpose "Blessed are the poor in spirit" "Kingdom, power, glory forever"	Jehovah Shalom (Peace) Sabaoth (Hosts)	Shoes of Preparation of Gospel of Peace	Leviathan	Unclean – Luke 4:32-33 Infirmity – Luke 13:11
Orange	Grace & Supplication	Zechariah 12:10 Hebrews 10:29	God's Promotion and Empowerment "Blessed are they that mourn" "Deliver from evil"	Jehovah Jireh (Provides)	Praying Always	Beelzebub	Man – Zech 12:1 Jealousy – Num 5:14
Yellow	Wisdom & Revelation	Deut 34:9 Ephesians 1:17 Isaiah 11:2	Progressive Insight and Application "Blessed are the meek" "Lead us, not into temptation"	Jehovah Rohi (Shepherd)	Shield of Faith Sword of the Spirit	Prince of Power of Air	Slumber – Rom 11:8 Error – 1 John 4:6.
Green	Life/Supply Prophecy Healing	Romans 8:2 Philippians 1:19 Revelation 19:10	Present Truth Rhema "Blessed are they that hunger and thirst after righteousness" "Give us daily bread / forgiveness"	Jehovah Rophe (Heals)	Helmet of the Hope of Salvation	Wormwood	Lying – 1 Kings 22:22 Divination – Acts 16:16
Blue (Light Blue)	Holiness Adoption	Romans 1:4 Romans 8:15	Saintliness / Righteous Purpose "Blessed are the merciful" "Thy Kingdom come, thy will be done"	Jehovah Mekaddesh (Sanctifies)	Clothed with Humility Breastplate of Righteousness	Anti-Christ	1 John 4:3
Indigo (Dark Blue)	God's Glory & Presence	1 Peter 4:14	Glory of God/ His Presence (Deleted from worldly depiction) "Blessed are the pure in heart" "Hallowed be thy name"	Jehovah Nissi (Banner) Shammah (God who is there)	Put on (enduo) Take unto you (anambulano)	Prince of this World	Bondage – Rom 8:15 Idolatry – Hosea 5:4
Violet	Truth : Son-ship	John 14:17 2 Timothy 1:7	Sons of God / Royal Commission "Blessed are the peacemakers" "Our Father in Heaven"	Jehovah Tsidkenu (Righteousness)	Loins Girt About with Truth Cloak of Zeal	Behemoth	Seducing – 1 Tim 4:1 World – 1 Cor 2:12

COLOR ONE: RED
THE SPIRIT OF JUDGMENT AND BURNING

Matthew 5:3   Blessed are the poor in spirit: for
theirs is the kingdom of heaven.

Jesus began His teaching known as the Beatitudes by declaring that the beginning step toward knowing God and entering into His Kingdom is to recognize the poorness of your spirit and the need for God.

The color red is the beginning point of the progression to the Father, and it is the culminating point of the visitation from the hand of God to the planet. Red has often been depicted as an angry and menacing color. In truth, it is the place that God affects His hand of reclamation and restitution, the position where life begins and ends.

Red is the color of upheaval and definitive change. How many times has the color red personified the flag of revolution? If someone is said to "see red," they are intent upon applying themselves in whatever measure necessary to right a wrong, or correct an injustice. Justice, or righteousness, is the way that God made things to be. In the spectrum of the Lord, red is the applied purpose of God. When the red blood of Jesus spilled upon the earth, the price for mankind and the planet was paid.

When you surrender to God, you must admit that life has no meaning without Him. As the repentant one, you find the point of submission to the purpose of God as your life is committed to Him.

By virtue of the red blood of Jesus Christ, scarlet sins are made as white as snow.

People and places must recognize the need for the Most High and for the institution of His pure purposes. Filth must be cleaned away in obedient anticipation of the visitation of the glory of the Lord. There must be a submission to this judgment and burning.

> Isaiah 4:4-6   When the Lord shall have washed away the filth of the daughters of Zion, and shall have purged the blood of Jerusalem from the midst thereof **by the spirit of judgment, and by the spirit of burning**. [5] And the Lord will create upon every dwelling place of mount Zion, and upon her assemblies, a cloud and smoke by day, and the shining of a flaming fire by night: for upon all the glory shall be a defence. [6] And there shall be a tabernacle for a shadow in the daytime from the heat, and for a place of refuge, and for a covert from storm and from rain.

When God visits the earth with His judgment, His sons will be entrusted with the power of judgment and burning. God will also grant to these conquerors a strength that is above the power of opposition.

> Isaiah 28:6   And for a **spirit of judgment** to him that sitteth in judgment, and for strength to them that turn the battle to the gate.

COLOR TWO: ORANGE
THE SPIRIT OF GRACE AND SUPPLICATION

> Matthew 5:4   Blessed are they that mourn: for they shall be comforted.

Once the individual has been touched by the repentance that initiates relationship with the Heavenly Father, the process of submitting to the Lord must begin. Mourning involves a reflection and release of the dying and dead, and our life must die and decrease so that Christ might increase within our lives. As Christ gave Himself for us, so we give ourselves for Him.

Grace is the manner in which God promotes us from one plane to the next. Additionally, grace is a mode of deliverance and promotion. God says in Hebrews 4:16 that we come before God's Throne of Grace. Literally, we approach God's Throne in repentance and in son-ship through the miracle of His mercy. God's Throne is made of grace, and it depicts His plan to promote us into the fullness of what He purposes for our lives.

> Hebrews 4:16 Let us therefore come boldly unto the throne of grace, that we may obtain mercy, and find grace to help in time of need.

Grace must be found, and it is a process. We are told to grow in grace, and that God's grace has seasons or dispensations. Supplication is a type of prayer and anointing that is essential for progressing in the steps of development that God has ordained for our path. Intercession is the first step after the prayer of repentance and must become the lifestyle of the believer. Supplication is necessary at each juncture within God's plan of development.

> Zechariah 12:10 And I will pour upon the house of David, and upon the inhabitants of Jerusalem, **the spirit of grace and of supplications:** and they shall look upon me

whom they have pierced, and they shall mourn for him, as one <u>mourneth</u> for his only son, and shall be in bitterness for him, as one that is in bitterness for his firstborn.

Grace must not be rejected or despised. Hebrews 12 tells us that God chastens every son that comes to Him. Those whom God loves will be continually in the process of dying. Paul died daily. John the Baptist decreased so that God might increase. We must adhere to the process of God for our lives.

Hebrews 10:29 Of how much sorer punishment, suppose ye, shall he be thought worthy, who hath trodden under foot the Son of God, and hath counted the blood of the covenant, wherewith he was sanctified, an unholy thing, and hath done despite unto the **Spirit of grace**?

Perhaps the unsung armament that is listed in the Armor of Ephesians 6 is that of praying always with all manner of prayer and graced supplication. When we begin to know the Heavenly Father, He will instruct us in His ways.

COLOR THREE: YELLOW
THE SPIRIT OF WISDOM AND REVELATION

Matthew 5:5 Blessed are the meek: for they shall inherit the earth.

Meekness is not weakness. Jesus was meek but certainly not weak. Meekness is the patient and wise application of knowledge and power. God grants this so that we might be His vessel upon the earth in glorious fashion.

Our walk begins at repentance and immediately initiates us in the upward pathway to the Heavenly Father. At each step, God reveals more about Himself and His ways. He is the impetus of all truth. Wisdom and knowledge can exist without truth being known. Some people are ever learning but never coming to the knowledge of truth (2 Timothy 3:7). This is why the Lord grants a belt of truth to gird up the areas of wisdom and knowledge.

> Ephesians 1:17   That the God of our Lord Jesus Christ, the Father of glory, may give unto you the **spirit of wisdom and revelation** in the knowledge of him:

Isaiah speaks of the mighty dimension of this spirit that would rest upon Jesus during His earthly ministry. Our Lord continually derived His energy and wisdom from regular intercessory times with the Heavenly Father.

Gold is a residual color of yellow. Our faith is likened to the refining of gold. When we apply and act upon the revelation and information that has been revealed to us, our faith is tried and we glean gold. Gold is a commodity of the overcomer, granted to those that faithfully and obediently apply what has been taught to them. Silver is the last alloy that is skimmed away during the refining of gold, which makes it a lieutenant or secondary color in authority structure.

> Isaiah 11:2   And the spirit of the Lord shall rest upon him, the **spirit of wisdom and understanding**, the spirit of counsel and might, the spirit of knowledge and of the fear of the Lord;

Wisdom and revelation will be gleaned through waiting upon the Lord. Counsel comes from listening intently. This devotion will yield might. Information and strength become wisdom and might through this process. The fear of the Lord is the beginning of wisdom (Psalm 111:10, Proverbs 9:10).

Individuals that are friends of God will be partakers of this divine wisdom. Moses personified this and was capable of imparting a measure of this enduement through the laying on of hands.

> Deuteronomy 34:9   And Joshua the son of Nun was full of the **spirit of wisdom**; for Moses had laid his hands upon him: and the children of Israel hearkened unto him, and did as the Lord commanded Moses.

COLOR FOUR: GREEN
THE SPIRIT OF LIFE, SUPPLY, PROPHECY

> Matthew 5:6   Blessed are they which do hunger and thirst after righteousness: for they shall be filled.

After we have accepted God, endured chastening and entered into the training of the Most High, we begin to be indoctrinated as sons of God. Jesus came to the Cross so that those who receive Him would have the power to become the sons of God. We are redeemed to the Father for that purpose.

It is in this dimension that we learn the privilege of being hungry and filled at the same time. Jesus leads us in the paths of righteousness for the sake of the purposes of the Father. Along this pathway we learn God's ways. We suffer to learn obedience in the usage of this power, just as Jesus learned obedience through the things He suffered. If we suffer with Him, we also reign with Him.

> Revelation 19:10   And I fell at his feet to worship him. And he said unto me, See thou do it not: I am thy fellowservant, and of thy brethren that have the testimony of Jesus: worship God: for the <u>testimony</u> of Jesus is the **spirit of prophecy**.

The Greek word translated as testimony in this terrific passage is *marturion,* or becoming a martyr. To give miraculous life to people, we must apply ourselves within this Spirit. The Word tells us that Jesus lives to pray for the Saints. He is praying for us to succeed in this process of development. Victory will grant dynamic effectiveness in applying God's entrusted power against the realm of sin and the power of death still entrenched upon the earth.

> Romans 8:2   For the law of the **Spirit of life** in Christ Jesus hath made me free from the law of sin and death.

This is not a Gospel of works or an admonition to pay a price for something that Jesus has already purchased. <u>This is all about entrusted and applied power.</u> Christians talk a lot about power, but there is very little of it in operation. This power is that which will change the world in the days and years to come. It will be our continual supply.

> Philippians 1:19   For I know that this shall turn to my salvation through your prayer, and the supply of the **Spirit of Jesus Christ**.

COLOR FIVE: LIGHT BLUE
THE SPIRIT OF HOLINESS AND ADOPTION

Matthew 5:7   Blessed are the merciful: for they shall obtain mercy.

When we come to the Throne of Grace, God will commence the process of grace or promotion. We obtain mercy in order to step into the places of God's commissioning. Mercy is an empowerment of energy and possibility. Those that followed King David were continually appealing for mercy and truth. In the life of Jesus, mercy was repeatedly requested by those that came to Him. As sons of God, we will be privileged to apply God's mercy to people and places. Mercy is not comprised of philanthropic enterprise. Mercy is not a band-aid. Mercy is an empowering and drawing force that leads to the fulfillment of God's grace-filled purpose for the human life and planet.

The Spirit of Holiness is literally a Spirit of Saintliness. The Saints are to be the embodiment of the Holy Spirit in ways beyond those of the general church. Many people have received the infilling of the Holy Spirit but have done little to proceed into active sonship Being born again is simply the beginning of our walk, just as being born into this world was our human beginning.

Saintliness is a calling that must be commissioned by dedication to the process of grace-filled promotion. Ideally, this wind guides and directs the process of development in Apostleship. It is here that Jesus leads us dynamically as our elder brother and first-born of many brethren.

Romans 1:4-7   And declared to be the Son of
God with power, according to the **spirit of
holiness**, by the resurrection from the dead: [5]
By whom we have received grace and
apostleship, for obedience to the faith among all
nations, for his name: [6] Among whom are ye
also the called of Jesus Christ: [7] To all that be
in Rome, beloved of God, <u>called to be Saints</u>:
Grace to you and peace from God our Father,
and the Lord Jesus Christ.

It is at this stage that we yearn for more of God and begin
to strive for intimacy with Him in a manner that is phenomenal in
scope and depth. We begin to call upon Him from the basis of the
purity within us. This is a call that appeals to our Father like no
other call. Perhaps this call is most admirably communicated
within the passage found in Zechariah 13. Those that endure the
process of refinement, coming forth as gold, will call upon God.
They will be as His precious people, and He will answer them as
such.

Zechariah 13:9   And I will bring the third part
through the fire, and will refine them as silver is
refined, and will try them as gold is tried: they
shall call on my name, and I will hear them: I will
say, It is my people: and they shall say, The Lord
is my God.

Romans 8:15   For ye have not received the
spirit of bondage again to fear; but ye have
received the **Spirit of adoption**, whereby we
cry, Abba, Father.

COLOR SIX: INDIGO BLUE
THE SPIRIT OF THE GLORY OF GOD – HIS PRESENCE

> Matthew 5:8   Blessed are the pure in heart: for they shall see God.

> 1 Peter 4:12-14   Beloved, think it not strange concerning the fiery trial which is to try you, as though some strange thing happened unto you: [13] But rejoice, inasmuch as ye are partakers of Christ's sufferings; that, when his glory shall be revealed, ye may be glad also with exceeding joy. [14] If ye be reproached for the name of Christ, happy are ye; for the **spirit of glory and of God** resteth upon you: on their part he is evil spoken of, but on your part he is glorified.

As we endure the chastening of the Lord and the refining of His fire, we become prepared to enter into His presence. The pure in heart will see the heart of God. There is nothing with which to compare God's glory. It is beyond enunciation of human tongue or type. This is the secret place of God's heart, the chambers of commune with Him. There is no earthly framework with which to define it further other than to christen it as the place of *Agape.*

Personifications of the rainbow by earthly organizations will often delete this color from the spectrum. The enemy wants to be like God, and He would just as soon remove the presence of God from the equation of the planet. Whenever you see a depiction of the rainbow that includes six colors, know that God has been excluded. In truth, many of the most corrupt organizations on the earth today have adopted the six-colored rainbow as their icon and standard.

Indigo blue is a thick and impenetrable color. The lighter blue of Holiness is a personification of a people that are becoming and reflecting this parenting hue. Even surrounding heaven itself, there is a darkness of this indigo variety. Those that pass from this life into eternity will penetrate this veil and suddenly be immersed into the glorious light of God. David speaks of this reality in Psalm 18.

> Psalm 18:11   He made darkness his secret place; his pavilion round about him were dark waters and thick clouds of the skies.

COLOR SEVEN: VIOLET
THE SPIRIT OF TRUTH AND SON-SHIP

> Matthew 5:9   Blessed are the peacemakers: for they shall be called the children of God.

There is no peace without war, no victory without conquering. If Jesus had already done all of our work for us, why would we be challenged to enter a *"peacemaking"* format? When we have seen God, we emerge with a measure of His truth that should be applied in order to set people free. We are royal representatives of His Throne. This is the Spirit of Son-ship and the Spirit of Truth.

> John 14:17   Even the **Spirit of truth**; whom the world cannot receive, because it seeth him not, neither knoweth him: but ye know him; for he dwelleth with you, and shall be in you.

The Comforter has been sent to us so that we will show forth what Jesus patterned during His earthly ministry. The greater works of which He spoke are ahead. Violet is a color of royalty that is a combination of red and blue. This speaks prolifically of our commissioning to apply the will of our Father upon His footstool, the earth.

> John 15:26   But when the Comforter is come, whom I will send unto you from the Father, even the **Spirit of truth**, which proceedeth from the Father, he shall testify of me:

The Spirit of Truth will set free. This Spirit will guide us into the pathways of God's purpose. The entire framework of the demeanor of this Wind is that of submission and humility. The color violet requires the highest amount of energy in order to be seen. The wavelength for this color is quick and concise thereby indicating efficiency and rapid response. In comparison to the large and unhurried pattern of red, violet is an enforcing medium while red is a signature of confident and circumspect outcome.

> John 16:13   Howbeit when he, the **Spirit of truth**, is come, he will guide you into all truth: for he shall not speak of himself; but whatsoever he shall hear, that shall he speak: and he will shew you things to come.

We are sent back into the world with the message of God's purpose to be applied therein. There is much spirit of error guiding the earth today, and it is a demonic spirit of powerful and twisting proportion.

> 1 John 4:6   We are of God: he that knoweth
> God heareth us; he that is not of God heareth
> not us. Hereby know we the **spirit of truth**, and
> the spirit of error.

It is at this point that opposition will come from the enemies of righteousness that populate the planet and the heavens. This is the return to the Tree of the Knowledge of Good and Evil. This time, the child of God will triumph. Consider the words with which Jesus concludes His Beatitudes.

> Matthew 5:10-12   Blessed are they which are
> persecuted for righteousness' sake: for theirs is
> the kingdom of heaven. [11] Blessed are ye,
> when men shall revile you, and persecute you,
> and shall say all manner of evil against you
> falsely, for my sake. [12] Rejoice, and be
> exceeding glad: for great is your reward in
> heaven: for so persecuted they the prophets
> which were before you.

This can be nothing short of outright warfare for the sake of righteousness. Contained herein is the manner in which the enemy will attack these mighty ones. Included in this list is accusation, reviling and persecution. The word in the Greek that is translated as evil is the word *rhema*. Literally, the enemy arm of the prophetic will begin to attack. We must not fear. We must not allow our mind to wither under the challenges of assignment and opposition. We must remain rooted and grounded in *agape*. We are the agents of righteousness.

> 2 Timothy 1:7   For God hath not given us the
> spirit of fear; but of power, and of love, and of a
> sound mind.

PROCEEDING FROM THE THRONE

As we continue in Jesus' teaching in Matthew 5, we arrive at the passages spoken of in the chapter entitled, "Viewing The Darkness And The Light." We are salt in the world. As we gather the seasoning of our Father for the place that He has planted us, we affect His bidding. If we do not, men will simply walk on us.

Look at what David says about coming from the presence of God.

Psalm 97:2-12   Clouds and darkness are round about him: righteousness and judgment are the habitation of his throne. [3] A fire goeth before him, and burneth up his enemies round about. [4] His lightnings enlightened the world: the earth saw, and trembled. [5] The hills melted like wax at the presence of the Lord, at the presence of the Lord of the whole earth. [6] The heavens declare his righteousness, and all the people see his glory. [7] Confounded be all they that serve graven images, that boast themselves of idols: worship him, all ye gods. [8] Zion heard, and was glad; and the daughters of Judah rejoiced because of thy judgments, O Lord. [9] For thou, Lord, art high above all the earth: thou art exalted far above all gods. [10] Ye that love the Lord, hate evil: he preserveth the souls of his Saints; he delivereth them out of the hand of the wicked. [11] Light is sown for the righteous, and gladness for the upright in heart. [12] Rejoice in the Lord, ye righteous; and give thanks at the remembrance of his holiness.

As we consider the concepts within the color spectrum from the perspective of God's Throne, we glean this process that David describes in the preceding passage of Scripture.

- As Royal sons, we proceed from the Father in order to accomplish His purpose and mission. Jesus continually said that He had to be about His Father's business. He stated "for this cause" on many occasions. Whatever He "saw" His Father do, that was what He taught and demonstrated. This is the mission of the Saint (Verses 2-4).

- The Spirit of Truth will guide us prophetically into the strategies of our God. He will grant wisdom and revelation, showing the places where grace needs to be manifested upon the earth. This grace application is for the purpose of bringing the earth and the people into proper alignment with the purposes of God for them (Verses 5-6).

- The Judgment of God and application of His truth will touch men, women and places. His glory will be revealed as we prepare the way for Him. Obstacles and mountains of demonic or geologic dimension will melt before His power and purpose (Verse 7).

- The Glory of the Lord will be revealed, and all flesh shall see it. This is the majesty that is spoken of in the Word, the resplendence that we have not yet witnessed upon the earth (Verses 8-12).

John the Baptist said that Jesus would baptize us with Spirit (Wind) and with fire. We become initiated into the things of the Seven Spirits of God until we are immersed in them. Then the fire of judgment and burning is applied to the place wherein we have been assigned.

The Saints are depicted as being clothed in bright white. This is indicative of the mantle of white light that comes from being submitted to the fullness of the colors of God. It is humility of major proportion, speaking of solemnity of purpose. Could this be the description of Jesus in the Epistle to the Colossians?

> Colossians 2:9   For in him dwelleth all the fulness of the Godhead bodily.

God offers to us the same privilege, honor and responsibility. If we think of our body as a reflection of the glory of God, and we are the Temple of the Holy Ghost, we align perfectly with the Seven Spirits.

THE PRAYER OF THE SAINTS

When Jesus taught His disciples to pray in the discourse found in Matthew 6, His progression of prayer flows directly from the Throne to earth in perfect alignment with the Seven Spirits.

As we view things from the perspective of our Father in heaven, we hallow His name and purpose. This is a place of abiding and becomes our very home. As we accept our saintly commission, we devote ourselves to accomplishing His will on earth as it is in the place of His purpose in heaven.

We flow dynamically in the Spirit of Life and Supply, gleaning every provision through the prophetic word of His heart. Our daily bread is provided as we hunger for His righteous supply.

There is no room for rejection or grudge, as we are not our own any longer. Everyone has their responsibility before the Father, and jealousy has no place.

Being led by the Spirit of Wisdom and Revelation will cause us to be able to not only prosper, but to avoid the areas of confusion that bring failure and defeat. The places that the enemy would attempt to trip us or trap us will become steppingstones of grace and promotion.

Reaching the place of judgment and burning will welcome and enlist the kingdom, power and glory into the earth. This transformation will be permanent, and forever we will rule and reign with Him. This is absolutely wonderful in scope. The ways of God are absolutely complete in every dimension.

GOD LOVES HIS WAYS

When we understand the ways of God that are clearly defined within His covenant for the earth, we can see these patterns everywhere in the Word of God. Perhaps no truer example of this can be found than that which is penned through the Prophet Isaiah.

Isaiah 59:9-17   Therefore is judgment far from us, neither doth justice overtake us: we wait for light, but behold obscurity; for brightness, but we walk in darkness. [10] We grope for the wall like the blind, and we grope as if we had no eyes: we stumble at noonday as in the night; we are in desolate places as dead men. [11] We roar all like bears, and mourn sore like doves: we look for judgment, but there is none; for salvation, but it is far off from us. [12] For our transgressions are multiplied before thee, and our sins testify against us: for our transgressions are with us; and as for our iniquities, we know them; [13] In transgressing and lying against the Lord, and departing away from our God, speaking oppression and revolt, conceiving and uttering from the heart words of falsehood. [14] And judgment is turned away backward, and justice standeth afar off: for truth is fallen in the street, and equity cannot enter. [15] Yea, truth faileth; and he that departeth from evil maketh himself a prey: and the Lord saw it, and it displeased him that there was no judgment. {16] And he saw that there was no man, and wondered that there was no intercessor: therefore his arm brought salvation unto him; and his righteousness, it sustained him. [17] For he put on righteousness as a breastplate, and an helmet of salvation upon his head; and he put on the garments of vengeance for clothing, and was clad with zeal as a cloke.

Notice the framework of the Lord within this passage. Darkness abounds as a result of iniquity and unrighteousness. Judgment is turned away from the places of darkness as righteousness is far removed from the land. The truth is not being applied and righteous people are preyed upon.

This entire scenario of depravity is not pleasing to the Lord, and He looks for someone to partner with Him so that His ways can be applied against the darkness. The eyes of God still look for an intercessor to affect this type of transaction upon the earth. When God finds such a person, the means of refinement and preparation are begun within that man or woman. These were the ways of God, and they remain before us today.

THE ARMOR OF LIGHT

Romans 13:12 tells us that we must put on the armor of light in order to cast off the ways of darkness. The holy armor of Ephesians 6 fits perfectly with the ways of God that are depicted in progression of His Seven Spirits.

When we know our Heavenly Father, we are cloaked with His zeal for righteousness, and we accept His truth that sets free. Truth is what girds our loins, and the loins guarantee strength and productivity. Fellowship with Him allows us to put on, or be endued, with every measure of equipping. We also take unto ourselves every weapon that He deems necessary for victory.

As a Saint, we are clothed with the white humility that embodies the desires of God and not our own. The breastplate of righteousness identifies who we are in God, as well as our commissioning and alignment for placement and service.

Prophetically we glean the hope of our calling. Firmly upon our head, the testimony of Jesus will cause us to continually glean the mind of Christ for our aim and goal. Wisdom and revelation will serve as our thought process training us in the words to say and the thoughts to think. Thinking rightly will cause us to not fall into the doubts and fears that wrong thinking creates. We are preserved from error and false steps.

Grace and supplication form the framework of prayer that continually leads us to our Heavenly Father. We recognize our ever-changing terrain and long for the promotion that only He can give.   When we walk in the dimension of conquering, administering the Spirit of Judgment and Burning, we will need the preparation of the gospel of peace upon our feet. Everywhere the sole of our foot treads, we will possess. Each battle will be different, and each place of conquest unique, so we are always preparing a new battle plan before our God.

TEMPLE OF THE HOLY GHOST

Location	Wind Color/ Spirit	Identity and Meaning
Top of the Head	Violet Truth, Son-ship	Crown of Royalty and Truth
Face	Indigo Blue Glory of God	Face to Face with the Glory of God
Shoulder	Light Blue Holiness	Saintly Commission and Ranking; Government upon the Shoulders
Upper Torso/Chest	Green Prophecy; Life	Our Identity as a Person and Minister
Lower Torso/Loins	Yellow Wisdom; Knowledge	Understanding; Strength of Belief; Productivity and Reproduction
Thigh and Knees	Orange Grace; Supplication	Promotion and Advancement; Strengthen the Feeble Knees (Climb)
Feet	Red Judgment; Burning	Victorious March of Conquest; Soles Tread and Possess

This is a fascinating insight and should bear careful consideration as we honor the Lord with our Body. God created the church in His image, and it is highly likely that individually we portray the dimension that is depicted above. This chart speaks of function, while the predominate color perceived on an individual or church speaks of purpose.

discerning
the colors

DISCERNING THE PROGRESSIVE COLORS OF THE WAYS OF GOD

Understanding the meaning of color is a powerful ally in the ministry of the Spirit. Granted, not every color is found in exact alignment with one of the seven colors of the rainbow, but all colors flow as hues of these seven.

It is sometimes helpful to judge colors by virtue of how they are formed, analyzing what colors join together to provide the chemistry of their make-up. Sometimes a person can analyze a scenario by virtue of the combination of colors involved. For instance, violet being formed by red and blue speaks volumes as to our mission and from whence it comes. The green of applied prophecy comes from saintly blue and the wisdom and knowledge of yellow. The red of applied purpose mixed with the wisdom and knowledge of yellow provide the way of grace-filled promotion found in orange.

Sometimes as I intercede, God will give me a vision of a scenario into which I am being sent to minister. I will witness colors on the spectrum that are prominent upon the landscape of revelation. When it is obvious that a connecting color is missing, I know that the missing color is perhaps more significant to the equation than that which is seen.

If I witness many hues of orange and green, but recognize that yellow is missing, there is a prominent need for revelation and insight. Information is required in order for grace to proceed toward provision, or for provision to find its way into promotion.

Once, I witnessed all of the colors of the rainbow, except for indigo blue. I knew that the church for which I was praying was suffering from the Ephesian syndrome. They had everything in place, but they had lost their first love, or the presence of the Father. I also knew that there was a prominent maneuvering of the antichrist spirit, either within the church or coming against the church. The antichrist spirit will attempt to stop the Saint from pursuing the Father.

At one point, I saw a brown wall, which is indicative of the world. Orange people and yellow people were trying to get through the wall. What they needed was the contiguous spirit of judgment and burning to be visited upon them and the place. This was either a need for perfect timing, an insight of *dunamis* points, or both.

Seers must be intercessors, or they will not be tuned in to the flow of God's heart. There are times when the only manner in which accurate interpretation comes is when those that speak the mysteries in an unknown tongue "pray that they might interpret." Interpretation will involve detail, timing and relationship.

DISCERNING THE COLORS OF PEOPLE AND THINGS

It has regularly been my delight to witness colors upon, around or within people. Shades and hues will often reveal their primary calling and commissioning. This can be very helpful in positioning people in the line of battle as a righteous formation on the left and right. It is helpful to become girded in an understanding of the color factors that are present on either end of

71

their spectrum placement. Additionally, it enables me to provide insight and counsel as to what these people need according to the dimness or paling of their color base.

There are times when people are seen with little or no color. This is usually indicative of a lack of ongoing relationship with God. The absence of color does not always imply that there is little going on, as it could simply mean that God is doing a secret work within the person, and it is none of my business.

The most troubling scene is that which involves black lines or spots. Lines are places wherein the enemy has infiltrated or where he is positioning upon a line of unresolved iniquity in the person. These lines are designed to bring division within and without. From our experience in the church that I pastor, it is rare that a person recovers from this malady as the only reclamation is absolute humility. Like roots of bitterness that spring up from failed grace, they will defile many that have known alignment with them in the past or present. Again, the safety of these peripheral ones is to remain in absolute submission to authority structure, responding in knowledge instead of emotion and employing the humility that is born through continual prayer.

Spots are more dangerous, as they indicate a double agent, or an individual that has been sent to infiltrate. Jude 1:12 speaks of those that are spots on feasts of charity. These individuals must be dealt with carefully but decisively.

Visions or dreams that are primarily in black and white are indicative of a line of demarcation between good and evil. Generally, this will depict a need for warfare or a pending battle for territory. Second heaven vision is often in black and white, as it portrays the conflict for dominion of a territory or dimension. Second heaven reality can be shown in vivid color, so do not accept a hard rule that this realm must be in black and white.

Shadowy visitations are regularly devoid of coloring and are sometimes difficult to interpret. Most shadowy spirits are not wholesome in intent. The shadow is regularly a lurking force bent on trickery or subterfuge. At times, your peripheral vision might register the movement of a spirit, and it might be indicative of the presence of a messenger from God. Invariably, the frontal visitation of a shadowy creature will indicate a force that is malevolent.

Holographic vision is an entirely different matter from that of a shadow. There are times that God will communicate to us in the form of multiple variations of sensory gifts. Holographic sight will often portray a multi-layered message that depicts various dimensions and time frames. Be wary of this approach, as it is a favorite of the dark realm.

Just as in a sales scam, a lot of commotion and variation can produce the confusion necessary to deceive. A flurry of activity can simply be a camouflage designed to mask the weaknesses of each individual facet.

DISCERNING THE COLORS OF NATIONS

The same type of principle can be applied to places. Churches, cities and continents will follow the same progressives of God's spectrum. It is wonderful to pray over a map of the world. One of the ways God will reveal His intent for the moment and future is by the imposition of color over the vectors of the map. When praying concerning a city, the Lord may convey upon a certain coordinate a dullness of a particular color. This represents either a deficiency of that influence within the city or a stronghold of enemy influence that is blocking a major storehouse within that place.

An intriguing thing to do is to analyze the flags of nations as to their color and symbolism, as this can tell you volumes about the nation. The United States is a land that has been visited by the red judgment of God on many occasions and has realized subsequent awakenings of white as a result. This is depicted on the right, or prophetic section of the flag. The line-upon-line process plays out in full on six progressions, but the seventh line of judgment is not heeded and accepted. In the upper left corner there is a square of indigo blue that depicts the presence of God. There are fifty stars within this square that correspond to the angelic host that will affect the destiny of each state. The left is that which brings a completion to the plan of God, and there will be a dynamic visitation of these angels in our days.

What of Canada? Red all around speaks of a prevailing and continuing measure of judgment and burning. It is no wonder that rebellion and secession is an ongoing discussion throughout most of that beautiful country. Everywhere, people speak of their inherent right of land and self rule. However, the blessing of God is apparent in the white leaf within the center. God blessed the world through Canada, and this land will be a resource of His visitation in the very midst of the seedbed of turmoil and revolution.

Mexico? Red, green, and white: This is a land that has known the same pattern of promise and disappointment for generations, a land of continual revolution and the false promise of provision. God will visit this country, and the green snake of false prophecy and divination will be destroyed by the eagle representing the Saints. There is great revival coming to Mexico. There will be open confrontation between the agents of righteousness and the enemies of righteousness.

Some flags were designed by artists and others by the collective passions of the people. The latter is most easily defined and prophetically interpreted. God holds great store in the banner that flies over a land or people group.

The flags of God's Saints, which are His banners of love, are most revealing in nature and prophetic insight. Each unit within the army of God will be overshadowed by a banner that relates His love for the people of that particular movement. There are colorful and intricate details upon these banners that depict the purpose and calling of these passionate warriors.

DISCERNING THE COLORS OF ANGELS

The angels of the Lord are an extremely colorful contingent. Each of the angelic tribes possesses their own distinct patterns and colorings according to their function and alignment. For instance, Gabriel and his contingent display vibrant garb of many hues, and when they move it is with a suddenness that is almost strobe-like in speed displacement. They leave a rainbow trail of light that marks their vacated path. The Selah angels are bright white and red in apparel. The angels of the Lord are almost always outfitted in brilliant white, radiating the presence and glory of the Most High. These are undoubtedly the consignment that moves in conjunction with the Saints. The angels are spirits, or winds, so it stands to reason that they would be colorful.

The brilliance of their appearance is because of their relationship with God. The term angel means "messenger," so it stands to reason that they are an embodiment of what God is both doing and communicating. Their appearance is a sign in itself. Without the privilege of relationship with God, the angels lack purpose and meaning.

Fallen angels will assume many types of shape and form. Those spirits that were of a higher ranking before the fall will display a dim visage of their former selves. Sometimes a fallen angel may be outfitted in remarkably similar clothing to that of an angel of God. The absence of the presence of God has deprived them of their former luster, and they display a dingy and blanched coloring.

Mind you, there are some enemy forces that are resplendent in appearance. The Bible says that gifts and callings from God are without repentance. In the case of some of the fallen angels, there is enough of the residue of the former glory to preserve their countenance to a large degree. There are power reserves in the enemy kingdom that can be tapped. Suffice it to say that just like any vain dictator, there are prideful leaders of the demonic realm that are going to make sure that they manifest in style.

The best that I can offer in this regard is that we must try the spirits (winds) as to whether they are of God. It is helpful to know that if you see a dingy spirit being, it is demonic or a representation of a dead work or move. Discerning the color of the being is helpful in that you can ascertain its specialization before the fall. This information can also help you in deducing the current mission of the being and what its assignment might be in the area.

Some locations on earth are like black holes in the spirit realm. There is a vast darkness and shadow that envelops these places, and it is very much like what is spoken of in the second letter of Paul to Corinth.

> 2 Corinthians 4:4   In whom the god of this world hath blinded the minds of them which believe not, lest the light of the glorious gospel of Christ, who is the image of God, should shine unto them.

A darkened atmosphere can also be a utilization of that which is present upon the earth from when the planet was originally created. This is the place within your city that has embodied a certain type of evil or debauchery for as long as anyone can remember. Similar to a haunting, no matter what generation, the corruption remains endemically the same. God created something in the master plan of the earth that has been unrealized or twisted at that location. Light must shine into these hidden places (*krupto*), and they must be turned for good. They will begin to manifest the goodness of God, and they will be changed into a position of glory.

Many of the fallen angels inhabit the terrain to which they were assigned before the fall. If you hold to the belief that fallen angels are spirits left over from a pre-Adamic race of people, it would still be plausible to assume that they would want to stay in the same locale where they lived. Remember the first case of deviled ham in the Bible when the spirits asked Jesus to send them into the swine so that they would not have to leave the region?

Three colors that the enemy loves to utilize are light green, pink and lavender. All three of these are a watering down of vibrant, power colors of the rainbow covenant. When the enemy lightens red, he states that judgment is really not going to come. After all, there is innocence and tenderness that is being communicated. Lavender mocks the strength of authority and the ultimate purpose of God. Light green offers a pleasant picture of prophetic ministry as well as false promises of provision.

Our Seers and intercessors regularly encounter the angelic. These messengers and warriors are prominent in the Bible, and in the moving of God's people today.

One of our intercessors is also a gifted artist. For the purposes of illustration within this book, I asked Isai Hernandez to depict an angelic scene from the Word of God in order that we might enjoy an exercise in interpretation.

In Figure 1.A (inside front cover), we enjoy a rendition of the *Ischus* angel in Revelation 10. *Ischus* is one of the powers of God, and these types of angels deal primarily with the purposes of

God upon a land. These mighty ones are assigned to each continent upon the earth and will work with the Saints in the establishment of God's visitation as detailed in eschatological passages of the Scriptures.

Notice the rainbow upon his head. This clearly speaks of his assignment and the intent of his purpose. This angel cooperates with the Winds of the Spirit in enforcing the covenant for the earth. He is surrounded by a cloud, which speaks of the Glory of God that will rain upon the land, a latter rain of harvest and miracles. His face as lightning speaks of a quickness of obedience to the Word of God. Lightning also speaks of that which will precede the earthquakes that come as a result of obedient intercession. His legs are as fire, which says that he comes to conduct the business of judgment and burning from coast to coast, aligning the land with God's purpose. The little book in his hand is the scroll of mystery that the saint and intercessor must make as their diet and source of sustenance.

There are many other things that could be discussed, but our focus is upon color and issuance of the same. From the brief depiction included herein, this angel becomes so much more than what our black and white, linear-based cognitive approach can provide. God is a God of color and variety.

DISCERNING THE COLORS OF THE BIBLE

While the recognition of color is a manner in which we can discern what God is doing within a person or a place, it is also extremely helpful in the interpretation of the Word of God. How many times have we encountered a description of color within the Bible and simply passed right over it? Probably most of the time, right? This should not be acceptable to the literalist. After all, as every Word of Scripture is inspired and inerrant, then the colors have to be, as well.

Granted, some of the colors defined within the pages of the Word are difficult to ascertain because of the antiquated nature of designation. It is difficult at times to really know which color is being described. While there is nothing that can be done about that, we certainly have no difficulty in dealing with the absolute colors.

- God Upon His Throne

There are scores of examples, and it is an illuminating process to read the Bible with the color chart at hand. Ask God to illuminate the moving of His Winds and ways at every place that a description of color is mentioned. Let us look at one of these in the Book of Revelation.

> Revelation 4:3   And he that sat was to look upon like a jasper and a sardine stone: and there was a rainbow round about the throne, in sight like unto an emerald.

In this passage, God is said to be sardine (brownish red) and jasper (reddish brown) in prevalent color. This means that His intent is the visitation of judgment and burning to the brown dust of earth. The rainbow of the earth surrounds the Throne as an artistic backdrop. Hence, this framework deals with the purpose of God for His footstool, the earth. His Throne is emerald (green) that speaks of the promotion and acquisition of prophetic application, life, supply and healing.

The finale of this scene occurs in Revelation 5 when the Lamb of God arises to take the Book of the Earth and is entitled to open it due to His victorious and complete sacrifice at Calvary. Truly, the death of Jesus visited the payment for God's reclaiming of the earth, and His testimony (martyrdom) forms the Spirit of all true prophecy. The Throne of God is depicted in many ways throughout the Bible. In Daniel 7:9, God is shown as sitting in white attire and appearance upon a throne that "was like the fiery flame, and his wheels as burning fire." This speaks of the judgment of God upon the Thrones of the earth. In Revelation 20:11 we behold "a great white throne," and this depicts a time to come when the fullness of God for the heaven and earth will once again be known by virtue of the completion of the institution of righteousness.

- Perilampo

In Figure 1B (inside back cover), one of the most magnificent scenes in all of the Word of God is found in the rendition of the birth of Christ that Luke relates in his Gospel. He provides a stunning depiction of the glory that attended the shepherds in the field of Bethlehem on the night when Christ was born.

Luke, whose name means light, reports that the angel of the Lord came to the shepherds in the power of the glory and obedience of the Lord. He came upon them, establishing the *histemi* of God as the glory of God shown round about them. The glory of God was revealed in a *perilampo*, or a light that shown all around in a complete display of the colors of God. Literally, the Seven Spirits of God came in richness; culminated by the light of the angelic proclamation to the shepherds.

Incredibly, the angel was joined by a multitude of the heavenly host that declared the fullness of the ways of God. This splendid group began by proclaiming the glory of God in the highest, or purple measure. To the earth, peace was declared as a depiction of the farthest application of red to the world and to men. The red blood of our Lord would first spill upon the earth and would then be applied to the people that would accept His sacrifice.

What a majestic sight this must have been for the shepherds! They were witnessing the fullness of the ways of God in the birth of the Lord Jesus. Not only did they witness this with their eyes, but they heard the message with their ears. They then obeyed and went to see the baby Jesus.

- The Ultimate Measure of Color: The Two Robes of Jesus

As a conclusion for this chapter, it would be wonderful to view something that is subtly depicted at the passion and crucifixion of our Lord.

Matthew 27:28-31   And they stripped him, and put on him a scarlet robe. [29] And when they had platted a crown of thorns, they put it upon his head, and a reed in his right hand: and they bowed the knee before him, and mocked him, saying, Hail, King of the Jews! [30] And they spit upon him, and took the reed, and smote him on the head. [31] And after that they had mocked him, they took the robe off from him, and put his own raiment on him, and led him away to crucify him.

John 19:2, 5   And the soldiers platted a crown of thorns, and put it on his head, and they put on him a purple robe, [5]   Then came Jesus forth, wearing the crown of thorns, and the purple robe. And Pilate saith unto them, Behold the man!

John 19:13   When Pilate therefore heard that saying, he brought Jesus forth, and sat down in the judgment seat in a place that is called the Pavement, but in the Hebrew, Gabbatha.

Color makes a great deal of difference in the Bible and in the story of our redemption. Apparently, Jesus wore a violet robe on the night that he was betrayed, and into the day of His crucifixion. This depicted His Kingly representation on behalf of the Heavenly Father.

The Soldiers removed that violet robe from Him, and placed a scarlet, or red, robe on Him. This act speaks of judgment and burning, and the finality of the visitation of God to reclaim His purpose for the earth. Before being led away, the soldiers placed the kingly robe upon Jesus once again. He went to the Cross as the King while Pilate sat as the representative of the earthly authority in the place of judgment.

Scarlet to Purple – the full spectrum of the rainbow as depicted in the mantles of our Lord!

viewing the darkness and the light

There are many studies embodying extensive observation concerning the application of color that are certainly admirable in scope. Additionally, there have been amazing pursuits in the field of light, both in medicine and other applied technologies. For the purpose of this writing, recognize that color and light are integral to an understanding of the spirit realm.

Artistically, we know that if all of the colors of a box of crayons were to be applied to the same spot on a page, we would create something very dark. Darkness results from the neglecting of individual purpose and responsibility. The dark will manifest in the false promise that implies an ability to do whatever, whenever and wherever you want. The enemy promises everything in the world, and that results in darkness.

The Lord Jesus said something in Matthew 6 that attests to this fact. The defining concept of whether we adhere to darkness or light is found in the measure of our spiritual eyesight.

VISION DETERMINES HOW LIGHT IS PERCEIVED

- Dark Light

Matthew 6:23   But if thine eye be evil, thy whole body shall be full of darkness. If therefore the light that is in thee be darkness, how great is that darkness!

Evil vision, simply explained, is that which is a twisting of the purpose of God. If the directive vision of the body is yielded to an undisciplined or self-serving intent, the end result is the darkness which encompasses everything. Darkness comes by virtue of the absence of light. Literally, darkness is the rejection of the light of God. Regular litmus of spiritual activity within the life of a human is observed by looking into the eyes. Although not always a foolproof test, it can regularly provide valid and ready indication of evil activity within.

The all-seeing eye of the occultic world is an eye that desires all things. This eye seeks for the pleasures of the world and turns from the light of God. This eye is indicative of the Babylonian system that has twisted the purposes of God toward a humanistic and demonic end. God's light will overcome this through the devoted light bearers of the Kingdom of Heaven. Perhaps the blinding of Elymas the sorcerer in Acts 13 was a demonstration of the terminating of demonic vision within that region. The god of the world who has blinded the eyes must first be bound.

Additionally, Wormwood is depicted in Revelation as being in appearance as a lamp. This demonic being that moves as a prophetic entity in witchcraft is obviously a false wind. Leviathan, or the King of the Prideful, is said in the book of Job to have the influence of a lamp in his mouth. In the time of the end, the enemy himself will manifest himself as a messenger of light. Each of the fallen hierarchy of the enemy was exceptional in major modes of service to the Lord. The Bible tells us that in the days to come, the enemy and his minions will transform themselves into a measure of light, and it will be quite convincing.

2 Corinthians 11:14-15   And no marvel; for Satan himself is transformed into an angel of light. [15] Therefore it is no great thing if his ministers also be transformed as the ministers of righteousness; whose end shall be according to their works.

This transformation is nothing new for the enemy and his cohorts. In fact, it is quite probable that the fallen ones were extremely efficient at manifesting the power of light by virtue of their gifting and training. The Bible tells us that Satan was perfect in all of his ways until iniquity was found in him.

Ezekiel 28:15-16   Thou wast perfect in thy ways from the day that thou wast created, till iniquity was found in thee. [16] By the multitude of thy merchandise they have filled the midst of thee with violence, and thou hast sinned: therefore I will cast thee as profane out of the mountain of God: and I will destroy thee, O covering cherub, from the midst of the stones of fire.

Perfection within the ways of God is an apt description of being able to transact the light and power of the Most High. Perhaps discretionary exercise of this dynamic power became such a regular occurrence for these fallen ones that they actually began to think that the power belonged to them. It is conceivable that the iniquity that was found within Satan was not necessarily pride but willfulness in the application of the ways of God. In other words, God allowed them such discretionary authority that they actually began to exercise it as their own – thus, twisting the power of God from the purpose of God, and that is iniquity. The merchandising and violence of Verse 16 is kingdom-taking languageListed within the framework of the provided color chart is the alignment of demonic entities that comprise the council of hell. These rebellious creatures once served God as angels of power and duty but now serve to emulate His light in the dark realm. Undoubtedly, they form the basis of the "seven more wicked" spirits that the dispossessed demon consulted in the account of Matthew 12. While this topic is covered in detail in the book <u>Princes,</u> it is imperative that we recognize that the enemy will_attempt to emulate the light of the Lord, and many will be deceived.

It is therefore essential that we be trained and dutiful, not being led about by natural appearance or by the notion of the crowd. In Matthew, we are told that some of the very elect will be deceived by false signs and wonders. Man looks upon the outward, but God looks upon the heart, or spirit. We must learn to do the same.

- White Light

White light comes as a result of the presence of all of the colors in the light spectrum. When each of us focuses our eye toward fulfilling our individual purpose in God, we align with our brethren in perfect form and experience the fullness of our God.

> Matthew 6:21-22   For where your treasure is, there will your heart be also. [22] The light of the body is the eye: if therefore thine eye be single, thy whole body shall be full of light.

A single eye! What a magnificent concept and truth! As we concentrate on what God has called us to be, fulfilling our role in Him, we will be filled with His light and presence. Wonderfully, the word for the light of the body in this verse is more readily translated as lamp *(luchnos)*. We will also enjoy the thrill of manifesting the beauty of the Lord in accordance with the colorful purposes of the Seven Spirits of God.

As this occurs, there will be a glow that is visibly seen upon the people of God and the places wherein they minister. Moses communed with God, and his face glowed to the degree that the common folk could not look upon him. Jesus came from the Transfiguration, and the Word of God tells us that His clothing glistened. When Stephen was being martyred, he lifted his face toward the heavens and his face glowed as that of an angel. In the days that are coming, we will pattern that which is prophesied in the Book of Isaiah.

> Isaiah 60:1-4   Arise, *shine*; for *thy light* is come, and the glory of the Lord is risen upon thee. [2] For, behold, the darkness shall cover the earth, and gross darkness the people: but the Lord shall arise upon thee, and *his* glory *shall be seen* upon thee. [3] And the Gentiles shall come to *thy light*, and kings to *the brightness* of thy rising. [4] **Lift up thine eyes round about, and see:**

JESUS PATTERNED THE PURPOSEFUL LIGHT

John spoke of the Lord Jesus at the beginning of his Gospel. Matthew and Luke were inspired to provide a witness as to the way that Jesus came into this world as a baby. Mark commenced his Gospel with the inception of the ministry of Jesus upon the earth. John preceded the accounts of Matthew, Mark and Luke by showing us the very form of God.

> John 1:4-5   In him was life; and the life was the light of men. [5] And the light shineth in darkness; and the darkness comprehended it not.

When light comes, darkness must flee. In our day, God grants us the opportunity of knowing Him as He really is – The Light. When His colors are seen in and through us, and they are applied into His world, the darkness will flee. We have the privilege of partnering with the Heavenly Father. Regularly in the Word of God we see a bright light that is associated with significant Kingdom events. God is light.

James admonishes us that we must not vary from that which God has called us to fulfill within His spectrum of light. The good and perfect will come as we adhere to the purpose and plan of God in this life. Variation from our calling will not do! Shadowy diversion from our reflection of Him and His ways is unacceptable.

> James 1:16-17   Do not err, my beloved brethren. [17] Every good gift and every perfect

gift is from above, and cometh down from the Father of lights, with whom is no variableness, neither shadow of turning.

Paul wrote to the church at Phillipi that we must not envy the calling of another, and that we must not argue for a change of our individual purpose.

Philippians 2:14-15   Do all things without murmurings and disputings: [15] That ye may be blameless and harmless, the sons of God, without rebuke, in the midst of a crooked and perverse nation, among whom ye shine as lights in the world;

To be blameless is to be true to color, and to be harmless literally means to be unmixed. We are sent to apply God's purpose into the midst of a crooked and perverse world that is languishing in the resultant darkness. We are the light of God's purpose and truth.

LIGHTS AND LAMPS

The ministry of the Lord Jesus was for the purpose of bringing men and women to the Heavenly Father. Without that ministry, nothing else matters. Without Jesus, we have nothing. With Him, we have the prospect of serving our Father upon this earth. The church has wrongly assumed that our mission as believers revolves solely around winning the lost and taking care of the many problems within the church. The business of manifesting God's light should continually be addressed to the planet and before the structure of the current world system. Consider this well-known passage that connects light and lamps.

> Matthew 5:14-16   Ye are the light of the world.
> A city that is set on an hill cannot be *hid*. [15]
> Neither do men light a candle, and put it under a
> bushel, but on a candlestick; and it giveth light
> unto all that are in the house. [16] Let your light
> so shine before men, that they may see your
> good works, and glorify your Father which is in
> heaven.

The Lord says that cities are to be addressed with God's eternal light. The word for hid in Verse 14 is the Greek word *krupto.* Superman fans will recognize that the fictitious material called kryptonite, or the substance from his home planet that rendered him powerless on earth, is a derivative of the Greek word *krupto.* This word means "the secret things within a place or person that form the facade that they hide behind." This word is utilized in 1 Corinthians 14:25 in regard to the places within the heart of an individual that are revealed through personal prophetic evangelism. These places are formed by the wounding and lies of the enemy, and God wants to shine the light of His purpose into them. People and cities have *krupto* that must be addressed and corrected. Just as God will prophetically address the *krupto* of a person, He will also prophetically address the places of darkness within a city. Peter affirms the truth of the lamp shining into a dark place.

2 Peter 1:19   We have also a more sure word
of prophecy; whereunto ye do well that ye take
heed, as unto a light that shineth in a dark place,
until the day dawn, and the day star arise in your
hearts:

Matthew 5 identifies this ministry as being directed to a
city or a place. To this place, God sends a candle that should more
properly be translated as a lamp. Remember that lamps signify the
Seven Spirits of God. In the context of Jesus' words, this lamp is
foolishly covered by a harvest basket. There is nothing wrong with
a harvest basket, unless of course, it obscures a lamp. If the church
disregards the ministry of the lamp, or Seven Spirits, by an over-
attendant concentration upon harvesting people or things, the city
will not be saved.

In the Gospel of Luke, Jesus addresses this same issue in
two additional ways. In Luke 8:16, the Lord warns against hiding
the lamp under an apparatus or a bed. The apparatus, or area of
our preferred interests, can hide the lamp of the Lord. To hide the
lamp under a bed speaks of the act of laziness. In Luke 11:33, the
Lord adds that the *krupto* of our own heart, the iniquity or twisted
places within, can seek to hide our ministry as a lamp of the Lord.

In the days to come, we will be privileged to witness the
spectacle of entire cities coming to the knowledge of the Lord God.
This will not happen through the brilliance of unique evangelistic
crusades. We have had these campaigns in abundance, yet the
cities continue to languish behind uncontested facades of

debauchery. We will win the city by the lamps of God shining into the secret places and prominent places.

From the teachings of our Lord, we clearly see the obstacles that will stand against the moving of the lamps of God. We must guard against the following adversaries to the moving of the Seven Spirits of God in the cities and continents of our world.

- Disregarding the Seven Spirits by preferring other necessary harvest ministries.

- Concentrating upon our own interests or the places in which we feel most comfortable and skilled. God will usually choose the thing that we feel we cannot do in order to showcase His Glory.

- Laziness

- Iniquity within our own life.

The city will then begin to manifest God's original intent for that locale as the lamps are manifested. The people of the city will then begin to see the gospel in clear fashion as the darkness of the prince of this world is removed from their eyes. This is end-time evangelism.

Jesus tells us in John 4:35 to lift up our eyes to a field that is *white* unto harvest. He is telling us to rely on the Seven Spirits of God for an evangelistic thrust instead of the timetable of traditional harvest method. The wisdom of man will not be able to predict such a mighty move of God.

As we obediently fulfill this mission, our lights will shine before men. People will see this work, and the Father will be glorified. When John was beholding the Father while in heaven, he was able to hear the message of the Father's heart. Our message is the same that John declared in his first epistle.

> 1 John 1:5   This then is the message which we have heard of him, and declare unto you, that God is light, and in him is no darkness at all.

When God created this world, it was full of light. The rebellion of Satan created darkness. When God looked upon the void of darkness in Genesis 1, He spoke His intention – LIGHT. Sound and light are based upon the same registry of expression. Therefore, God spoke and shined light at the same time. This mandate continues to guide His intent for the planet and for us.

As the children of light continue to partner with the Heavenly Father, the stage is set for a glorious appearance of the Lord Jesus. In the last words of the Holy Spirit in the Old Testament, we are told that the brilliant Sun of Righteousness is going to be seen upon this planet.

> Malachi 4:2   But unto you that fear my name shall the Sun of righteousness arise with healing in his wings; and ye shall go forth, and grow up as calves of the stall.

As He arises from the east, His arms of power, healing and restitution will stretch forth as rays of light. This arising is already beginning, and it will precipitate many climactic visitations in the natural and spiritual realm. A Sun can only mean one thing, and that is brilliant light and fire. It is the light and fire of righteousness, typifying the ways of our God.

THE LAMP WILL SHINE NO LONGER

In Revelation 18, we witness what will happen to the world system that rejects the lamp of the Saints and Prophets. God's rainbow covenant with Noah stated that the earth would never again be destroyed by water. Another type of destruction is to come.

> Revelation 18:23-24   And the light of a *candle* shall shine no more at all in thee; and the voice of the bridegroom and of the bride shall be heard no more at all in thee: for thy merchants were the great men of the earth; for by thy sorceries were all nations deceived. [24] And in her was found the blood of prophets, and of Saints, and of all that were slain upon the earth.

Note that the candle, or lamp, will no longer shine within this city and world system. The voice of the Bride and Bridegroom will no longer be heard therein. Saints and Prophets will have already shed their blood for the cause of Christ. The appeal of God for a return to Him will be concluded as His timetable for this planet draws to a dramatic culmination.

This seems like a morbid conclusion to a glorious prospect. We must remember that God specializes at moving suddenly in the midnight hour. The day begins at the darkest hour. When the enemy crucified our Lord Jesus, darkness covered the earth. It appeared that the light had been extinguished. In the same way, the light will triumph in the last day. God, who spoke light into the darkness in the beginning, will triumph once more in the end. John the Baptist declared the way and was martyred, then the Son of God came upon the scene. Judgment prepares the way for glory.

CHANGED INTO HIS RADIANT LIGHT

When the earth has been changed into the brilliance of God's original purpose and intent, the beauties of eternity will be known by those who have served Him in this life. According to Revelation, the Lord Jesus will be our continuing light, and we will absolutely become a part of Him. We become partakers of His fullness, or white light.

> Revelation 21:23 And the city had no need of the sun, neither of the moon, to shine in it: for the glory of God did lighten it, and the Lamb is the *light* thereof.

> Revelation 22:5 And there shall be no night there; and they need no *candle*, neither light of the sun; for the Lord God giveth them light: and they shall reign for ever and ever.

What a glorious day that will be!!!

the 7 resurrection of the seer

The enemy is training both children and adults to flow in the dark forces. It would seem that the church is the only group that has not fully realized that the spirit realm is more real than the natural. One of the strategies of the enemy is to keep the people of God from moving in the visionary giftings that God has given them. Satan will use religious means to tell the Seer that the obvious gift within them is not for today, not normal, or inherently demonic. Subsequently, the visionary gift will remain dormant or will be utilized in the camp of the unrighteous.

God is awakening the Seer and the Prophet. They are to be the eyes and ears of the army of God. If the people of God do not stand up for the sensory gifts that God has given, the church will lack vision and will perish. The forces of hell have fought against these facets of insight more than any other. In warfare, a blinded foe is an easy target that is lacking in maneuverability and aim, and not prone to the strategy of conquest.

The enemy will tolerate a church that is content to sit and wait. He does not mind a church that studies victories of the past in a nostalgic manner. The enemy is quite comfortable with the people of God having head knowledge of the Bible, as he possesses that as well.

What Satan does mind is a group of people that see what God sees, visionary people that know demonic encampments and can expose hiding places and lies. People with vision and commission are a frightful thing to him. This is reminiscent of when Saul was made to be the king over Israel. Immediately, the enemy king of the Amonnites wanted to blind the right eye of the

the resurrection of the seer

men of Jabesh-Gilead. The right eye symbolizes the prophetic and is important in any scheme of vision. Saul was enraged at this terrible prospect and furiously arose to defeat the enemy strategy. Those that will reign as kings before God must arise today to defeat the blinding strategy of our enemy.

How Was The Seer Withdrawn?

Apart from the enemy hating the Seer, he could not single-handedly remove this facet from the church. He had to have help in this pursuit, and he found it in religion. Religion does not like open vision because it challenges the comfortable status quo. A trait of mankind is that we are prone to finding a resting place and staying there.

If you are a settler instead of a pioneer, you do not need a trail guide. This is especially true if you are the Mayor of the town and do not want to lose constituency. Spiritual insight that is revealed to multiple sources can be a problem point for insecure leadership. Most problems within the church are the result of a power struggle for control, and this is usually a first-round opponent of any new move of God. Unless the leader is devoted to God and open to the moving of the Spirit, the Seer will most likely be unwelcome in a local church.

Speaking purely from a pastoral perspective, having Seers in your church requires a lot of work for the leader. The Pastor must develop a Scriptural structure wherein the words of vision can be judged properly. This involves a network of praying people that are totally committed to God and His ways. It also requires uncommon humility and deference to each other. Seers and their leaders have to remain vulnerable and in submission to the authority structure in order for things to be as they should. In short, it is much easier to pastor a church without Seers, but not nearly as much fun.

The church is often more concerned with being deceived than with trusting the voice of God. One of our Seers was ministering to a young man that had been beset by the demonic. God gloriously delivered this fellow, and he happily returned to his home with a glowing testimony of deliverance. Imagine the shock of this young man when later he was told by another seasoned minister that discerning the presence of angels was a psychic tool and that he needed to question the freedom that he was enjoying. This tale is reminiscent of the man that Jesus healed who told detractors, "whereas I was blind, now I see" (John 9:24).

REJECTION: PREREQUISITE OF THE SEER

Many Seers have been wounded or rejected in some way because of their gifting. Often, individuals such as these compensate by adapting a victim mentality in their spiritual life. This makes them extremely difficult to deal with, especially if you are trying to lead them. For these, the only thing they have known from authority is betrayal and rejection. Spiritual wounds run deep and are hard to heal and retrain. Just as the Levites were not permitted to minister while their body recovered from any wound, the curative process must be given appropriate time.

You might say, "I was wounded in such a terrible manner that I do not think I can ever really be set free. I have a right to carry this badge of rejection, as I do not ever want to be hurt again." Let us consider the life of Samuel for an example of how God will take care of the rejected Seer.

Samuel was a miracle baby. When he was barely old enough to know anything, he was given away by his loving mother. Many psychological theories are based upon such themes of maternal dysfunction and deprivation, yet Samuel was somehow preserved. Adding to the perils of the young child was the fact that he lived a Cinderella-like existence in some ways. Eli, the dim-visioned High Priest, had two raucous sons named Hophni and Phineas. It seemed that little Samuel did most of the work while the privileged sons of Eli lived a life of wantonness.

If anybody had a "right" to rely on his wounding, it was the Prophet and Seer called Samuel. Instead of latching onto his plight, Samuel pursued God. Many times what is labeled as a reaction to "wounding" is really accusation against somebody or against God. The recipient of the wound is looking for some type of restitution or vengeance. Invariably, this type of pursuit ends up being a question of how God could have allowed this to happen to you.

The enemy will target individuals from the time that they are born into this world. Possible generational gifting is known by virtue of observing the ancestry over a period of decades before the birth of the little one. Additionally, the dominant gifting within a person can be seen through the color dynamics within and upon them, even in infancy. If these dynamics are not properly understood, they can prove to be a continual source of challenge for the individual who has them. The enemy will attack this anointing in any way possible.

Here is the strategy of the enemy. If he can create a wounding through some source, he can begin to twist the individual toward his camp. He knows the wounding since he created it, and he uses the resultant rejection and rebellion to draw the unsuspecting one to his side. Often the anger and hatred toward the earthly source of the pain will serve as a springboard into the realm of darkness. These children of disobedience get that way because of a rebellion that was engendered by the enemy, or by the ostracism that resulted because of their resident gifting.

This strategy of the enemy is probably one of the factors that Jesus addressed when He blessed the children. If there was ever an individual that understood rejection and misunderstanding, it was Jesus. He was in all points tempted as we are, yet without sin. Our Lord is moved by the things that have wounded us.

Let us consider the life of David, the youngest son of Jesse. The Bible says that he was conceived in iniquity, banished to the outer fields as a shepherd. Samuel arrives at the home of Jesse in order to anoint a king, and David is considered an afterthought. Eventually David is anointed as king, and he immediately finds himself back in the obscurity of the fields. Before the triumphant battle against Goliath, the brothers of David call him names and question his motives. After the defeat of Goliath and a string of successive victories on behalf of the king, David's life is threatened by the king that he had just valiantly served.

What about Joseph and his brothers? How about Joseph and Potiphar? Joseph possessed so many Seers giftings that he wore a coat comprised of many colors. Consider John the Baptist. The list goes on. God allows rejection and wounding within the lives of Seers and other notable people to reveal what they are made of inside.

Some Seers are not wounded but are just plain prideful and cocky. There is little submission within them, because they "have the answers." There is a power issue with them, and they love to tell the leader every fault that "God" reveals. This type of behavioral pattern requires a dose of humility with continual booster shots. It also belies a twisting of the Seer's true role in regard to a leader; that is, a source of information and tactical option for the Body to which they have been assigned.

Every individual within the church should be active in spiritual perception. Unless there is an understanding of the role of the Seer and an acceptance of that ministry, the Seer will find a hard time fitting into the "normal" church. All of these factors weigh heavily against the role of the Seer being welcome and functional.

THE SEERS OF HELL

The Word of God tells us that many of God's people would prefer to live a gentle existence. Therefore, God has granted them the desires of their hearts. There has been an unspoken covenant with hell that says, "we will leave you and the spirit realm alone if you leave us alone." Isaiah speaks of this in graphic detail.

> Isaiah 28:15   Because ye have said, We have made a covenant with death, and with hell are we at *agreement*; when the overflowing scourge shall pass through, it shall not come unto us: for we have made lies our refuge, and under falsehood have we hid ourselves:

In this passage, the Hebrew word translated as agreement is the word *chozeh,* which is the primary word for Seer in the Old Testament. Literally, a complacent attitude toward spiritual things is not just a choice, but an agreement with hell. Tragically this brings the church under the unwitting influence of the counsel of hell and it leads to death and destruction.

The resultant attitude toward legitimate Seer and prophetic gifts is nothing short of demonic. Two chapters later in Isaiah, the Lord says something that sounds remarkably like our churches today.

> Isaiah 30:9-10   That this is a rebellious people, lying children, children that will not hear the law of the Lord: [10] Which say to the Seers, See not; and to the prophets, Prophesy not unto us right things, speak unto us smooth things, prophesy deceits:

Subsequently, God allows the people to be lulled into a catatonic state, neither dead nor alive. This placid state is not acceptable to the Lord, and He tells us in His Word that He will vomit lukewarmness out of His mouth. The mouth is the prophetic

source, and any course of ambivalence to the spirit realm is
unproductive and repulsive to Him.

> Isaiah 29:10   For the Lord hath poured out
> upon you the spirit of deep sleep, and hath
> closed your eyes: the prophets and your rulers,
> the Seers hath he covered.

THE DAYS OF ELI: THE HIGH PRIEST

There is good news for the church! God knows how to
remedy dormant vision. He can still raise the dead and open the
blinded eye. He did this during the days of Eli by the introduction
of Samuel, the Prophet and Seer.

> 1 Samuel 3:1   And the child Samuel ministered
> unto the Lord before Eli. And the word of the
> Lord was precious in those days; there was no
> open vision.

No open vision. Sound familiar? The word of the Lord is
always precious, but it should not be rare. God wants His people
to be filled and hungry at the same time. He desires that the sons
and daughters prophesy, and that the young men see visions while
the old men dream Godly dreams. This is the promise of Pentecost
and the last day church. In essence, these are the missing gifts of
Pentecost. Thankfully, God knows how to deliver what He has
promised.

A praying woman named Hannah called unto the Lord for
life within her. She was like the modern church in many ways.

Hannah enjoyed a happy home and was married to a loving and considerate husband. God put within her a desire for miraculous provision. He is doing that in the hearts of intercessors all over the world. Like Hannah they look foolish to the religious establishment but remain undaunted in their prayers for life.

God is going to answer the prayers of these intercessors. He will give birth to the Seers and Prophets that the Kingdom of God is waiting to receive. Samuels are being born even now. Consider the words of Amos, the Prophet and Seer.

> Amos 7:12-15   Also Amaziah said unto Amos, O thou Seer, go, flee thee away into the land of Judah, and there eat bread, and prophesy there: [13] But prophesy not again any more at Bethel: for it is the king's chapel, and it is the king's court. [14] Then answered Amos, and said to Amaziah, I was no prophet, neither was I a prophet's son; but I was an herdman, and a gatherer of sycomore fruit: [15] And the Lord took me as I followed the flock, and the Lord said unto me, Go, prophesy unto my people Israel.

Here is a news flash. Bethel is not the chapel of earthly authority. It is not the court of mankind. Bethel is the House of God. The Most High is going to speak through His people. Like Amos, God is raising up individuals from all walks of life that are gifted as Prophets and Seers. There are individuals that are currently using their God-given gifts within the kingdom of darkness. God is going to reclaim and redeem these people in ways similar to that of Saul on the Damascus Road. He may choose to grant a dream to a Seer like Ananias for the purpose of arranging ministry to this type of individual.

SIGNS AND WONDERS

Miracles, signs and wonders will occur in accordance with the way that God is moving in the hour. When we align ourselves with His current move, signs will broadcast that message in spectacular form. This would serve to explain the continuing question as to why miracles are readily reported among ministries that go into obscure places but do not regularly populate the established places. Simply, God reserves incredible signs to accompany those that are patterning the demonstration of His fresh ways.

Jesus speaks about this in Matthew 16, beginning with a rebuke of the pharisaic system.

Matthew 16:1-4   The Pharisees also with the Sadducees came, and tempting desired him that he would shew them a sign from heaven. [2] He answered and said unto them, When it is evening, ye say, It will be fair weather: for the sky is red. [3] And in the morning, It will be foul weather to day: for the sky is red and lowring. O ye hypocrites, ye can discern the face of the sky; but can ye not discern the signs of the times? [4] A wicked and adulterous generation seeketh after a sign; and there shall no sign be given unto it, but the sign of the prophet Jonas. And he left them, and departed.

The Lord classifies these religious bystanders as hypocrites because they want signs in a manner that is not linked to why God gives signs and wonders. Jesus says that colors in the sky are readily interpreted to predict weather conditions, but the *kairos* moments around these individuals are unheeded. Later in this chapter, the Lord warns His disciples against the leaven, or fervency, that causes that type of hypocritical religion to be so dangerous. Leaven of hungering for entertainment and self-gratification is a hazardous element in the spirit realm.

As an aftermath to this episode and to the feeding of the thousands, the Lord provides an incredible insight regarding the ways of God and the power that enforces their display. When He and the disciples are crossing the Sea, Jesus inquires whether they brought food for the journey. Mind you, He has just fed the thousands and rebuffed the sign-seeking Pharisees.

As the men attempt to answer the Lord, Jesus makes a startling statement in Matthew 16.

> Matthew 16:8-10   Which when Jesus perceived, he said unto them, O ye of little faith, why reason ye among yourselves, because ye have **brought** no bread? [9] Do ye not yet understand, neither remember the five loaves of the five thousand, and how many baskets ye took up? [10] Neither the seven loaves of the four thousand, and how many baskets ye took up?

Jesus uses the word *lampo,* meaning lamp or shining, to describe the possession of miraculous bread. Literally, God is saying that when we partner with His winds, or lamps, there will be a miraculous display that provides for the crowd, and for the minister. This is an amazing promise and truth.

Signs follow those that believe. It is a matter of what we believe. If we believe the signs that God provides – the signs of the times and the colors of His wind – all things will be possible as signs will follow us. God will have His Seers and Prophets. The covenant with death is being annulled.

the seer in action

THE PROPHET AND THE SEER

In the previous chapter, we discussed Samuel. Perhaps this would be a good time to dispel a common misconception regarding the Seer. Many people will read the following verse and wrongly assume that the advent of the Prophet made obscure the Office of the Seer.

> 1 Samuel 9:9   (Beforetime in Israel, when a man went to enquire of God, thus he spake, Come, and let us go to the Seer: for he that is now called a Prophet was beforetime called a Seer.)

Samuel was a Prophet and a Seer because the dearth of spiritual acuity in the land demanded that he fill both offices. Within this chapter, we witness many examples of Seer ministry that occurred during the reigns of many of the kings of Israel. The inception of prophetic ministry did not make obsolete the Office of Seer.

Even today, there are those that serve as both Prophet and Seer. This happens for several reasons and can easily transpire since the Prophet and Seer are destined to flow perfectly together. The Seer provides a wealth of information and insight. The Prophet sees as well but is more inclined to decisive assessment and proclamation. They flow alongside each other like an artist needs art supply and a scholar requires a library.

In the New Testament, the Seer most likely became the Office of the Teacher. In Acts 13, the Teachers and Prophets combined to launch the Apostolic mission of the church. This is the way things ought to be in our churches today. Teachers should be alive in the Spirit, providing understanding in Spirit and in truth. Like bastions of spiritual resource, they should serve the body in humility. This was the Office of Seer and still is today.

THE SEER DEFINED

The word most commonly utilized in the Old Testament to portray the Seer is the Hebrew word *chozeh.* This powerful description means "to agree, to compact with or to behold." The Seer was generally aligned with a leader, a movement or a revelatory progression, enhancing the visual capacities in the spirit realm for the leader or nation. Is it any wonder that the enemy has sought to form a wedge between the Pastor and the Seer?

It has been said that an obituary most fittingly describes what a person should have been rather than what they actually had been. If you could choose the person that would write your obituary or eulogy, whom would you select? Would you select someone that hated you or who would be inclined to misrepresent your character? Most likely you would elect someone who believed in you, who knew the things that you faced and overcame, and someone who loved and supported you regardless of what had opposed your way. In this light, view some Scripture with me to see who was selected to write the life eulogy of some of the kings of Israel.

1 Chronicles 29:29   Now the acts of David the king, first and last, behold, they are written in the book of Samuel the Seer, and in the book of Nathan the prophet, and in the book of Gad the Seer,

2 Chronicles 9:29   Now the rest of the acts of Solomon, first and last, are they not written in the book of Nathan the prophet, and in the prophecy of Ahijah the Shilonite, and in the visions of Iddo the Seer against Jeroboam the son of Nebat?

2 Chronicles 12:15   Now the acts of Rehoboam, first and last, are they not written in the book of Shemaiah the prophet, and of Iddo the Seer concerning genealogies?

God did not deem it necessary to preserve the books of Seers such as Gad and Iddo, or the books of Prophets like Nathan, Shemaiah or Ahijah. Nonetheless He allowed these individuals to write the epitaph of kings. This speaks of the close relationship of the Seer and the King.

Seers were devoted to the leader because of their gifting and calling. They were committed to the cause of God, submitting to His chosen leader. Like political advisors from the Lord, they provide insight and option to the king. Once delivered, the leader can then assimilate and utilize what the Lord has made available.

THE HAZARDOUS CONDITION OF THE LONE PROPHET

As a leader, I continually desire the input of our Seers. As they behold, agree and compact what they perceive, I am provided with a palate of incredible vistas of understanding. The gathering together of Seers will enhance the overall spiritual atmosphere of the Body. Allow me to insert a word of wisdom concerning the application of this process.

Remember that God is the one that aligns the configuration of Pastor and Seer, as well as the authority structure involved. The Seer must never force their gifting and input upon an unwilling or unwitting leader. If the leader is not desirous of this type of ministry, do not attempt to force it. All things must be done in proper order and timing.

God did not mean for the Seer to abide alone. As iron sharpens iron, the senses and abilities of Seers are greatly enhanced by the alignment with others of similar gifting. Humility and submission are essential to this process as the enemy will attempt with all of his energy to infuse competition and jealousy into the mix, knowing this tactic will be a strong deterrent to his unholy agenda.

From this productive alignment, the Prophet can spring forth in mighty ways. The king and kingdom are benefited greatly. This is undoubtedly why there were schools and enclaves of Prophets throughout the kingdom of Israel. Whenever you witnessed a lone Prophet or Seer, it generally meant that the kingdom was in bad condition.

Lone Prophets can be a danger to themselves and to the places to which they visit. Often, the circumstances that led to their isolated condition can be a blinding and infective influence to their well-being and message. For this reason, I am generally wary of the uninvited and unknown Prophet that visits my congregation, especially when they desire to give me a "word." The Bible tells us that we must know those that labor among us.

This does not preclude the possibility that God can add a word from an unexpected source. The point is that He generally grants a prophetic word through the system that is established in His Word. Just as in anything else, the fruits of the person will dictate the nature of the tree. A legitimate Prophet will humbly and respectfully deliver a word to leadership.

Even when David committed the adulterous and murderous act with Bathsheba, Nathan came with respect to the king. Additionally, God did not send a chorus of rogue Prophets to inform the king concerning the error of his ways, but chose to send the king's Prophet to him. God will always respect His own authority structure.

If God's appointed leader has a system of prophetic insight, God will provide a word in due season and in a respectful and gracious manner. What if we do not think that God appointed the leader? God respects the office as much, or more, as He does the person that inhabits the office. When Paul was speaking accurate words to the Jewish leadership in Acts 23, he immediately changed his course of action and declaration when he recognized the Office of the High Priest, Ananias.

> Acts 23:4-5   And they that stood by said, Revilest thou God's high priest? [5] Then said Paul, I wist not, brethren, that he was the high priest: for it is written, Thou shalt not speak evil of the ruler of thy people.

This Scriptural principle dictated the actions of the great Apostle even after the New Covenant had eradicated the validity of the earthly Office of the High Priest. How much more should we respect that which God desires to employ today!

THE SEER TO THE KING

The connection between King and Seer is a powerful principle that is observed throughout the Old Testament. The king is reliant upon the insights that God would provide through the office of His anointed and illumined ones.

King Saul began his ministry by seeking for a Seer. This pursuit was in regard to lost livestock belonging to Saul's father, but the standard is clearly established. Seers provide Godly answers that resolve riddles. Seers provide direct and clear words that assist in processing and ascertaining a situation. King Saul relied upon such direction from God.

> 1 Samuel 28:6   And when Saul enquired of the Lord, the Lord answered him not, neither by dreams nor by Urim, nor by prophets.

Saul was so desperate for this necessary ministry that he wrongfully went so far as to consult the witch of Endor concerning needed information. Certainly, the kings of Israel needed the Seer.

In the life of King David, there were trusted voices of prophetic insight. David relied upon signs and directives from God throughout his life. Even when he failed with Bathsheba, Nathan the Prophet was there with him. When David sinned in numbering the people, Gad the Seer was with him. Gad respectfully provided options from God in the face of incredible judgment upon the king and the kingdom.

> 1 Chronicles 21:9-10   And the Lord spake unto Gad, David's Seer, saying, [10] Go and tell David, saying, Thus saith the Lord, I offer thee three things: choose thee one of them, that I may do it unto thee.

Perhaps the most aligning word concerning King, Seer and the Seven Spirits of God is found in the following passage:

> 2 Chronicles 16:7-10   And at that time Hanani the Seer came to Asa king of Judah, and said unto him, Because thou hast relied on the king of Syria, and not relied on the Lord thy God, therefore is the host of the king of Syria escaped out of thine hand. [8] Were not the Ethiopians and the Lubims a huge host, with very many chariots and horsemen? yet, because thou didst rely on the Lord, he delivered them into thine hand. [9] For the eyes of the Lord run to and fro throughout the whole earth, to shew himself strong in the behalf of them whose heart is perfect toward him. Herein thou hast done

foolishly: therefore from henceforth thou shalt have wars. [10] Then Asa was wroth with the Seer, and put him in a prison house; for he was in a rage with him because of this thing. And Asa oppressed some of the people the same time.

To King Asa, God sent Hanani the Seer. Note the respect of the Seer for the King, and observe the rational counsel that is provided for the leader. Asa had been a pious and good king, but needed to rely on the ways of God a bit more. Hanani lends his word toward that end, ministering to this flaw in the character of the king by reminding him of God's faithfulness in the past. Asa eventually would die because he did not trust the faithfulness of God in regard to the needs of his own body.

In this instance, Asa did not "receive" the words of the Seer. In fact, the Seer was punished for his obedience to God, but the Seer must always remain humble. Within the words of Hanani to Asa, note the emphasis that is lent toward the Eyes of the Lord. The Seer will focus upon the ways of God, and the moving of His Seven Spirits. As this mandate is honored, the Seer will remain successful in the face of acceptance or rejection.

THE SEER AND THE ADMINISTRATION OF THE TABERNACLE OF DAVID

According to the Words of God found in Amos 9:11 and Acts 15:16 the church is to be patterning the Tabernacle of David. It would be prudent to observe the role of the Seer within this important prophetic venue.

King David relied upon the Seer and Prophet in order to institute the vital ministry of establishing porters and gatekeepers within the House of God. These individuals were crucial to the ongoing business within the Tabernacle. Literally, they conducted the ebb and flow of daily administration and operation.

Today, we would perhaps review a resume and hire the person with the best qualifications to run the physical plant of the church facility. We also might entrust the appointment of leadership to a committee or a board. David relied upon a Prophet and a Seer in order to assess and appoint these important tasks.

> 1 Chronicles 9:22   All these which were chosen to be porters in the gates were two hundred and twelve. These were reckoned by their genealogy in their villages, whom David and Samuel the Seer did ordain in their set office.

What would happen if we were to relegate the appointment of all church offices to that of the Seer and Prophet? How would it change things within our churches? How many "power people" would we lose because they were removed from position and influence? How much closer would our churches be to the heart of the Father?

We seem to have it backwards. The spiritual ones should be providing direction to the church. The main emphasis should be upon becoming more aligned with the Spirit and less aligned with the machination of the thoughts of man. Instead, the cognitive ones direct the church and try to keep the spiritual ones from becoming too noticeable. This hampers the development of the gifts of God within the church.

THE SEER AND WORSHIP IN THE TABERNACLE OF DAVID

The Bible tells us that Gad and Nathan were used by God to institute noisemakers in the hands of the Levites. Talk about an Act of God!!! No matter how you view it, a cymbal is a noisy thing. Not only were the Priests commissioned to allow this type of instrumental expression, they were constrained to personally pattern and administer the apparatus. Can you envision modern church leaders with cymbal, psaltry and harp in their hands? I cannot imagine which might be more of a stretch, the Seers actually having the power to commission this behavior or the Priests adhering to it.

Additionally, the three men that actually led the worship within the Tabernacle of David were classified and identified as Seers. Asaph was the chief Seer, and ministered primarily from a vocal standpoint. Heman was an excellent instrumentalist. Jeduthun seemed to be more suited to louder and more boisterous apparatuses of worship.

What they played was not as significant as the fact that they saw and desired to see. Granted, the musicians of the Tabernacle were skilled and were proficient at what they offered to the Lord. Instruments must prophesy, and musicians must be inclined to the streams of sound that are always within the heart of God.

Is there a Seminary anywhere in the world that includes within its curriculum a course on how to be a Seer? What if every candidate for a degree in music ministry had to first be shown to be a Seer? Look at the resume of David's worship leaders as cited in the Bible.

> 2 Chronicles 29:25   And he set the Levites in the house of the Lord with cymbals, with psalteries, and with harps, according to the commandment of David, and of Gad the king's Seer, and Nathan the prophet: for so was the commandment of the Lord by his prophets.

> 2 Chronicles 29:30   Moreover Hezekiah the king and the princes commanded the Levites to sing praise unto the Lord with the words of David, and of Asaph the Seer. And they sang praises with gladness, and they bowed their heads and worshipped.

> 1 Chronicles 25:5   All these were the sons of Heman the king's Seer in the words of God, to lift up the horn. And God gave to Heman fourteen sons and three daughters.

> 2 Chronicles 35:15   And the singers the sons of Asaph were in their place, according to the commandment of David, and Asaph, and Heman, and Jeduthun the king's Seer; and the porters waited at every gate; they might not depart from their service; for their brethren the Levites prepared for them.

It is obvious from a study of the Word that the ministration of the Seer was not solely endemic to the reign of David. Solomon continued in the same vein as the Temple was constructed. Even in the cited passage concerning the reign of Hezekiah, the principles of the Seer were observed.

God allowed Asaph to write several Psalms. To glean a picture of the heart and passion of this Seer, read Psalms 50 and Psalms 73-83. The insights and ardor for God are apparent in every utterance. There is no more powerful word than that which comes from the interpretation of the heart of God.

Seers within the present Tabernacle of David are going to be intent upon communicating the cadence of the beating of God's heart. These mighty ones will be explorers of the sounds of heaven, attempting to interpret these magnificent strains into an understandable framework. We must press the edge of faith in our music and worship. The Seer must be given the time to wait upon the Lord. Time for the selah must be provided so as to allow for the bridge of devoted utterance to cross between prophetic promise of purpose and its fulfillment.

These Seers are said to have been outfitted in white linen in 2 Chronicles 5:12-14, and this is the righteousness of the Saints according to Revelation 19:8. To capture the full measure of the sound of heaven is the glory of the Seer. This will be shown in the brilliant radiance of God upon the Saints and Seers that declare His mighty ways.

knowing the ways of God

The most important lesson that can be learned by the believer is that which involves the ways of the Lord. Three men personifying this maxim were Abraham, Moses and David.

ABRAHAM – THE FRIEND OF GOD

Abraham was a Seer. He was so much inclined to the ways of God that he was called the friend of God. In other words, God shared His divine life with this man. The virtue that God loved about Abraham was that he would believe anything that God said or showed him.

> James 2:23   And the scripture was fulfilled which saith, Abraham believed God, and it was imputed unto him for righteousness: and he was called the Friend of God.

> Genesis 18:17   And the Lord said, Shall I hide from Abraham that thing which I do;

Subsequently, the Lord allowed Abraham to see and know what He was going to do. Even the issuance of righteousness was shown in a most unusual setting.

> Genesis 15:5-6   And he brought him forth abroad, and said, Look now toward heaven, and tell the stars, if thou be able to number them: and he said unto him, So shall thy seed be. [6] And he believed in the Lord; and he counted it to him for righteousness.

128

> Genesis 15:17   And it came to pass, that, when the sun went down, and it was dark, behold a smoking furnace, and a burning lamp that passed between those pieces.

It is apparent that Abraham was a man of unusual spiritual character. The factor that empowered this virtue was that Abraham would believe the vision of the Lord. He lived His life in spirit; although, his promise was for the land upon which he journeyed.

MOSES – FACE TO FACE WITH GOD

> Exodus 33:11   And the Lord spake unto Moses face to face, as a man speaketh unto his friend. And he turned again into the camp: but his servant Joshua, the son of Nun, a young man, departed not out of the tabernacle.

Moses was a magnificent testament of patience. Here was a man who was absolutely honed in the face of the Lord God. The word of God says that the acts of God were shown to the children of Israel, but Moses learned God's ways.

> Psalm 103:7   He made known his ways unto Moses, his acts unto the children of Israel.

God is not interested in people who will cooperate solely with His acts. He is intent upon those who want Him and His ways. From them will flow the might and power of the Kingdom of Heaven. This concept is born out in the Book of Amos, the Seer.

129

> Amos 3:7   Surely the Lord God will do nothing, but he revealeth his secret unto his servants the prophets.

The Bible says that patience is the first sign of the apostolic.

Patience can be viewed in many ways. Sometimes people consider that the exhibition of patience is simply for the purpose of demonstrating how much we want something. There is a much deeper truth involved. Patience is that measure of waiting before God that allows His wisdom and might to be added to His existing revelation to us. Patience is a virtue, and it develops wisdom as well as devotion.

If ever there was an Old Testament Apostle, it was Moses. Here he is, roaming on the backside of the desert. I suppose if there is a worse place than the desert, it would have to be the backside of the desert. He had undoubtedly seen Mt. Horeb and witnessed many intriguing signs coming from that holy site. In Deuteronomy, Moses recounts that the angel that appeared to him in the burning bush had made residence within that site, as the Hebrew word translated as dwelt means "to recurrently appear, make permanence within, or become a regular dimension within a place."

> Deuteronomy 33:16   And for the precious things of the earth and fulness thereof, and for the good will of him that *dwelt in the bush*: let the blessing come upon the head of Joseph, and upon the top of the head of him that was separated from his brethren.

One day, Moses determined to invest himself into what he had regularly perceived. The Bible says that when God saw that Moses went over to look, He spoke to him.

> Exodus 3:2-4   There the angel of the Lord appeared to him in flames of fire from within a bush. Moses saw that though the bush was on fire it did not burn up. [3] So Moses thought, "I will go over and see this strange sight--why the bush does not burn up." [4] When the Lord saw that he had gone over to look, God called to him from within the bush, "Moses! Moses!" And Moses said, "Here I am."

Two lessons leap forward at this point in time. Moses was a patient individual that was not immediately moved by what was occurring around him. When he sensed the time was right, he responded. As Moses acted, so did God. Seers must wait upon the Lord and not be skittish with what they are registering. When the time is right for moving, they know it. We plainly see the friendship of God in action.

DAVID – THE LOVER OF GOD

King David possessed the wonderful blend of warrior and lover, and this reveals the two sides of both the heart and sword of the Saint. These two are forged together by the patient devotion to God. The problem with King Saul was his impetuousness which sought to please the people at the expense of waiting on God. The Lord found David, a king that would wait upon His heart.

> 1 Samuel 13:14 But now thy kingdom shall not continue: the Lord hath sought him a man after his own heart, and the Lord hath commanded him to be captain over his people, because thou hast not kept that which the Lord commanded thee.

Everything about David was powerful. While displaying strength in battle he was also able to win the hearts of friend and enemy alike. His greatest virtue was in waiting upon and loving God.

David demonstrated this patience in the institution of something called the selah. This term is found seventy-four times in the Scriptures, in the Psalms and in Habakkuk. The western mindset has neutered this dynamic spiritual concept. The selah was the personification of the ways of God.

Situated between the stated purpose of God and the fulfillment of that promise is a lengthy period of time. There always seems to be a wilderness connecting the promise to the fulfillment. Usually, there are days within that wilderness that make it seem as if both you and God made a big mistake somewhere.

God will have various strategic moments, *kairos* moments, that mark turning points within that buffer period of selah. The job of the Seer is to glean the time frame with patience, wait for the juncture points, and hold on for the fulfillment. Find any example in Scripture of someone doing a great work for God, and you will be able to identify the selah.

God calls intercessors to this place of stretching. A gap or valley could easily be an interchangeable word for selah. Wilderness could be another descriptive for this powerful concept. God tells us in Psalm 23 that He is with us in the valley, and this place is the connective pathway between mountains. It has been said that the journey is everything. The hunger for the goal is the most rewarding part of life. Pursuit is delight. An intercessor lives for the valley just as the warrior longs for war. God seems dearest in the valley. More moves of the Spirit have been stopped by success than by all of the machinations of hell combined.

This is why we must learn to be hungry for righteousness even when filled. Paul said that he knew how to be both full and hungry. When the reaper is in full operation, the plowman must be vigilant to keep on overtaking for the planting of the next harvest. God loves the valley. Many of His finest works were wrought within the valleys of the Scripture.

David knew well this waiting period. He faced it from his days as a shepherd boy throughout the rough days in the Cave of Adullam. It was during these waiting times that David proved his devotion to the heart of God. The Lord saw to it that there was always a son of Zeruiah around to test that waiting period, but David patiently stood strong. These were also times that David learned how to sing and praise the Lord while waiting upon the fulfillment of the promises of God to him.

The selah took several different forms and could last for several days at a time. These were times of waiting upon God in intercession and worship, song and demonstration of devotion to

God. This was not the twenty minutes of obligation during song service that the modern church calls worship. This was open devotion, a waiting upon God. This is the brand of ministry that is to be offered in the Tabernacle of David.

LEFT AND RIGHT

If we were to view the progression of the ways of the purpose of God on a scale, they would progress from right to left. This is the manner in which the Hebrew Scriptures were written and read, and it is the way that God reveals Himself to us. Most of us think from left to right, and the Word tells us that our ways are not the ways of God.

Within the Bible, the right is shown to be the prophetic telling of the purpose of God. The left is to be the fulfillment of that purpose. The Bible tells us that God's glory will rise in the east and will progress westward, just as our sun rises and sets from right to left. When the Sun of Righteousness arises with healing in His wings, He will do so from east to west, or right to left. The Lord Jesus arising with the Saints of Righteousness will come to reverse the ways of man and the twisted things of the enemy, restoring the righteous purpose of God. In our vernacular, the word righteousness begins with right.

The men of the Tribe of Benjamin were known for being left-handed. This tribe was almost destroyed because of the influence of Belial that pervaded their camp. Belial insists upon getting things NOW, doing things in the manner that is most pleasing to the flesh. The prophetic influence should focus upon what God says rather than what things appear to be. The days of small beginnings are usually the manner in which God initiates His greatest works. This is not to say that the left is evil, but that it must be coordinated with the proper cadence. Jesus was given a seat at the right hand of the Father upon His triumphant resurrection from the grave. He is the Spirit of Prophecy, and it was from this place that He accepted the call to come to the earth as fulfillment of the plan of the Father. It is also from this place at the right hand of the Throne that He directs His Saints in prophetic measure. At the judgment, the sheep will be gathered to the right and the goats to the left.

In modern cinematography, when something enters the scene from the right it is generally a good influence. An entity that appears from the left will most likely display ominous or suspicious intent. The prince of the power of the air obviously is well aware of this spiritual principle of demonstration and persuasion, so he utilizes it within his propaganda machine.

We need both the right and the left to bring an issue to completion. Our effective coordination of this will ensure our dexterity and effectiveness. The Lord instructed both hands to allow the other to do its own work. He specifically said that the left hand should not be informed or consulted about the activity and intent of the right. If you allow the left to control or influence the right, the works of God will not be fulfilled through those hands.

Matthew 6:3   But when thou doest alms, let not
thy left hand know what thy right hand doeth:

Perhaps this is shown forth most notably in the church at
Antioch. In Acts 13, the Teachers and the Prophets came together
to send forth the Apostles. This is perhaps the most crucial
phenomenon of the church world. Getting the Teacher and Prophet
to agree on anything is nothing short of a miracle, unless, of
course, the Teacher fulfills the Office of a knowledgeable Seer. In
our Western thought, the Teacher would be pragmatic and left-
oriented, while the Prophet would be of the right.   In the
framework of God, the Teacher would grasp the vision of the right
while the Prophet would materialize this reality and declare it
toward the measure of existence.

An additional insight is that people greet one another with
the right hand. To offer the left, barring a physical handicap, is an
insult. When striking any accord with another group of believers,
make certain that the pact is based upon prophetic inclination and
not for the convenience of prosperity or pride.

THE PROGRESSION OF SAINTLY INTERCESSION

Within the framework of the ways of God and the covenant
for the earth, we note one other wonderful truth regarding God's
ways. It has to do with the value of intercession and enunciated
worship in the process of God.

Revelation speaks of a pattern that is continually happening
in heaven. The procession from earth to heaven is this: voices,
thunderings, lightnings and earthquakes.

Revelation 8:5   And the angel took the censer, and filled it with fire of the altar, and cast it into the earth: and there were voices, and thunderings, and lightnings, and an earthquake.

Revelation 16:18   And there were voices, and thunders, and lightnings; and there was a great earthquake, such as was not since men were upon the earth, so mighty an earthquake, and so great.

God will cause His people to hear His voice that calls them to action and to devoted service. The Word says that God seeks for an intercessor to stand in the gap. In this case, it is that gap of selah between His purpose for the earth and the eventual fulfillment of the purpose.

The voices of the intercessor and worshipper will combine with that of heaven to affect an atmospheric shift, characterized by thunder. Just as in climactic conditions on earth, thunder signifies a clashing of two opposing fronts. Matthew 11:12 says that the Kingdom of Heaven suffers violence, and the violent take it by force. This is a determined and impassioned insistence of the will of God being done, and the atmosphere of heaven being welcomed. Thy Kingdom come is our voice as we prepare the way of the Lord.

Lightning follows as a display of the quick strike forces of God. His Saints are His children that move mightily and immediately to do His instructed bidding. Angelic representatives display the lightning-like obedience and efficiency of the Lord, and they are undoubtedly a part of this partnership of the fulfillment of God's will.

The final stage is earthquakes, which demonstrate the shaking of the earth and heaven in order that the things that cannot be shaken will remain. Earthquakes change the terrain forever. The dividing of the time, the land and the dimensions of God is characteristic of the last days.

THE DIVIDING OF TIME

A powerful insight is found in the words of the angel to Daniel in his seventh chapter.

> Daniel 7:25   And he shall speak great words against the most High, and shall wear out the Saints of the most High, and think to change times and laws: and they shall be given into his hand until a time and times and the dividing of time.

This is different terminology than what is found in Daniel 12. In that passage, there is a ready reference to a time period of three and one-half years wherein the Saints will openly do battle with the forces of the antichrist. In Chapter 7, the word for dividing is the Hebrew word *peleg.*

You might recognize this as the name of a man who was alive at the dividing of the planet and people at the judgment of the Tower of Babel, the inception of the Babylonian world system. God intends for us to know that there will be earthquakes of time and place during the days in which we live. There are at least five major earthquakes listed in the Book of Revelation. Derivatives of *peleg* include that which also speaks of rivers and gold.

God's people are going to know the measure of earthquakes in every dimension of their lives. It will be crucial for us to recognize the distinctives that are found within the time frame of God.

As was the case with the Rainbow, there is a reciprocal progression leading to God as well as leading back from God. Observe this four-fold succession coming from the Throne toward the earth.

> **Revelation 4:5**   And out of the throne proceeded lightnings and thunderings and voices: and there were seven lamps of fire burning before the throne, which are the seven Spirits of God.

Those at God's Throne with Him will prophetically see the resultant change characterized by the earthquake. From that vantage, the heart and purpose of God is communicated in reciprocal format: lightnings, thunderings and voices. What a God we serve!

It is imperative that the Seer knows the ways of God. These must be patiently learned, and our devotion must be rooted and grounded in His love. Myriad numbers of people will be blown about by every *wind* of doctrine. Some will run to and fro looking for what appears to be Christ. The true Seer and people of God will know Him and His voice, and another they will not follow.

10
the wind and the bride say "come"

FATHER, BREATHE WITHIN ME

Ultimately, the measure of the hand of God upon mankind is for the purpose of developing partnership with Him. The heart of our Heavenly Father is that we unite as one with our Lord Jesus to accomplish righteousness in the kingdom.

Allow me to present a wonderful prospect from a largely unheralded passage of Scripture from the Book of Galatians. Within these verses we find the incredible plan of God that is outlined within this discussion of seeing and breathing His winds and ways.

> Galatians 4:1-7   Now I say, That the heir, as long as he is a child, differeth nothing from a servant, though he be lord of all; [2] But is under tutors and governors until the time appointed of the father. [3] Even so we, when we were children, were in bondage under the elements of the world: [4] But when the fulness of the time was come, God sent forth his Son, made of a woman, made under the law, [5] To redeem them that were under the law, that we might receive the adoption of sons. [6] And because ye are sons, God hath sent forth the Spirit of his Son into your hearts, crying, **Abba, Father**. [7] Wherefore thou art no more a servant, but a son; and if a son, then an heir of God through Christ.

Most Biblical scholars will say that the usage of the word *Abba* in this passage is simply a term of endearment, similar to saying "Daddy." *Abba* expresses commitment of purpose before the Father whom we serve. Jesus invoked this term when He was in the Garden of Gethsemane in Mark 14:36 and submitted Himself to the cup of Calvary. Paul aligns this designation in Romans 8:15 when he speaks of the Spirit of Adoption or Saintliness. The point of all three usages within the New Testament is to say, Father, I commit to your ways and purposes.

The root of the word a*bba* is found in a Hebrew word that means "to breathe the purpose of God." Utilized fifty times as a root word, *abba* gains the meaning of being close enough to the Heavenly Father that you actually breathe His passion and intent. It is easy to understand that in some cultures this is a term of great endearment. Let us explore some of the fifty usages of the Hebrew word *Abba* in the Old Testament.

- Covenant With The House Of David

2 Chronicles 21:7 Howbeit the Lord *would* not destroy the house of David, because of the covenant that he had made with David, and as he promised to give a light to him and to his sons for ever.

Here is a powerful verse that aligns much of what we have discussed within the pages of this book. The Tabernacle of David displays the covenant of the ways of God for mankind and will depict these purposes by the light of God.

- Covenant For The Earth

Isaiah 1:19 If ye be *willing* and obedient, ye shall
eat the good of the land:

If you willingly breathe the ways and intents of the
Heavenly Father and discern them in their proper application, you
will harvest and devour the *towb* of the earth. Obedient is the
Hebrew word *shama*, a name of Jehovah meaning that God is here.
So as we breathe the breath of God, we come into His presence in
oneness.

Once again, we discover the idea of realizing the original
and perfect intent of God for this planet. The *towb* is that good
purpose that God wanted Adam to discover, implement and enjoy in
Eden. When God breathed His voice in the *ruach* of the day, this is
what He intended for man.

Since Eden, God has been searching for those that will
partner with Him in this way. His *abba* covenant extended through
the ages of the patriarchs. Perhaps no finer illustration of this can
be found than in the admonition of Abraham regarding finding a
wife for his firstborn son, Isaac.

Genesis 24:8   And if the woman will not be
willing to follow thee, then thou shalt be clear
from this my oath: only bring not my son thither
again.

In this passage, Eliezer represents the Spirit of God in the
pursuit of finding a bride for the son of promise. The Lord Jesus

desires a partner that will breathe His ways. There is no shadow of turning in the Divine offer, and the inclination of God has not altered throughout the ages. God desires a joint heir that will breathe His ways in oneness with Him.

Returning to Galatians 4, we must see that Jesus came to the earth in order that a joint heir could be found. When we decide to become more than a baby in God and commit ourselves to the acceptance of walking as a son, God will send the Spirit of Jesus into our heart in a fresh and dynamic manner. The text declares that this is subsequent to salvation.

When the Spirit of Jesus enters our heart, He begins to cry "Abba, Father." In no uncertain terms, Jesus is praying that the ways of the Father would be breathed through us: His winds, His purpose, His light – all that His covenant entails. Mankind was created for this mighty intention. The unique thing about the word "spirit" is that it is integrally connected with men and women. The Spirit of God, Wind of God and Breath of God are essentially the same thing. Humanity was created as a spirit, or wind, being.

We dwell in a body that is essentially comprised of water. Amazingly, a person can produce a singular rainbow simply by allowing their spirit to shine through their body. The blood within our veins is composed of essentially the same qualities as that of light. We have been given the privilege of being able to vocalize sound unto the Lord. Light and sound basically consist of the same thing, registering on different ends of a mutual continuum. The DNA registry of our voice is different than anyone else anywhere in the world. Our song and our light are unique in all of the creation of God.

An emphasis upon the winds of the Spirit of God and a concentration upon the light and color of God should not be an odd thing for us. God is light, and we are created in His image. Is it any wonder that in the last chapter of the Bible we read that the Spirit and the Bride say "Come!" This statement has to be a reference to the Bride of Christ and the Winds of the Spirit aligning for the purpose of welcoming the Lord Jesus Christ at the end of all things concerning our present world.

THE CORNERSTONE

As the Saints of God now have the privilege of partnering in powerful ways with the Seven Spirits of God, one would have to think that it is time for the chief cornerstone to be revealed. Jesus is that cornerstone, and He is represented as having seven eyes.

> Zechariah 3:9 For behold the stone that I have laid before Joshua; upon one stone shall be seven eyes: behold, I will engrave the graving thereof, saith the Lord of hosts, and I will remove the iniquity of that land in one day.

Each time that Jesus revealed Himself to the world there has been a rejection by the very ones that should prize Him. Who would dream that the builders would reject the apex of their work? This is unconscionable, but it will occur again according to the Word of God.

Psalm 118:22   The stone which the builders refused is become the head stone of the corner.

In this hour, I pray that the people of God will not reject the One for whom they are waiting. May the Lord help us to see Him and may we partner with Him in accordance with His Divine purpose. The season ahead will be one of great deception as the forces of darkness will be immense in proportion and magnitude. There will be a large falling away from the truth, and many will follow after the wrong voice. We must know His voice, and the time to learn that precious sound is now. As we do this, we will not follow any other voice.

God is raising up a people that will be skilled in the same manner as was Daniel. This man was a Seer, and he was shown the things of our time. He was told to seal up scrolls until the time of the end, and we are about to enter further into those days. In order to understand these scrolls and partner with God in the fulfillment of them, we must possess the "excellent spirit" of Daniel.

The Seer is crucial for the hour. Seers that will grasp the prophetic insight of the heart and purpose of God and who will write that vision to make it plain are essential. The Prophet will declare and pronounce this message into life and vitality. The Apostle will receive and apply the new things of God to the lands and people of the earth. The Evangelist will embody the explosiveness of the Lord, manifesting the miraculous as a magnificent strike force. The Pastor will oversee, fuel, and gird the troops for battle.

This is the way of God. It was in the days of Elijah and it still is the way of God. The Seer is hearing the sound of the abundance of the latter rain. Some are even seeing the cloud that is the size of a man's hand. We will soon see that hand manifested as the hand of Almighty God upon this earth.

Study. Pray. Believe God. Find your place in Him and submit yourself therein. Even so, come quickly, Lord Jesus!

recommended reading

BOOKS FOR SAINTS

Divers Tongues   By Ronald W. Crawford

The author, a seasoned pastor, takes us through God's Word as he unveils the strategic communication tool of divers tongues. This long hidden and misunderstood gifting brings spiritual warfare victories that are both wondrous and compelling.

Hierarchy   By Ronald W. Crawford

The realm of the spirit operates according to a precise structure of authority. Clearly depicted in the Bible, this organizational pattern is implemented within the Kingdom of God and the kingdom of the enemy. Doctrines of devils and the traditions of religion have kept these principles hidden, and the church has suffered as a result. The author unveils the Biblical patterns of authority that govern heaven and earth, as well as the release of power that flows from them. A must read for intercessors and those engaged in spiritual warfare.

Pneumatikos   By Ronald W. Crawford

As Priests of the Most High, the Pneumatikos minister before the very Throne of God. It is their privilege to communicate the secrets of the Kingdom to a church that is hungry for more of God. These spiritual ones are the Kings and Priests of the Book of Revelation, and will proclaim the mysteries of God to this world.

Princes   By Ronald W. Crawford

Our enemy is Satan, but he does not fight alone. The Bible directly identifies many evil rulers with which the church must contend, each with very specific tactics and purpose within the kingdom of darkness. The author describes several of these beings from the vantage point of the Word of God, as well as from direct encounters with them. Let us not be ignorant of any of the devices of our enemies.

Seers Catalog   By Ronald W. Crawford

God is awakening the office of the Seer. The Spirit of God is revealing many things in these days to those whose ears and eyes are opened. Learning how to utilize your senses will serve you in knowing how to be a proper steward of the mysteries of God.

The Saints
By Ronald W. Crawford

Jesus is rising with His Saints to conduct the battle of the end times. The forces of righteousness are being called and commissioned at this time. The King of Saints is searching for people who will follow Him in battle. Discover how to be one of God's mighty men and prepare for war!

Ministering with Angels
By Paul David Harrison

One of the distinguishing characteristics of the culminating events in God's timetable will be the influx of the angelic in our churches and individual lives. They are coming at God's bidding to impart gifts and anointings reserved for these last days. (Also available in Spanish)

Ministering from our Heavenly Seats
By Paul David Harrison

Scripture says God has "...made us sit together in heavenly places in Christ Jesus." The author describes what it is really like to pray and minister from the seats of authority God has purposed and prepared for His Son's bride, the church.

TOPICAL STUDIES FOR SAINTS

Dreams & Visions
By Ronald W. Crawford

The missing gifts of Pentecost are those which allow for communication with the most High at all times of the day and night. Consider the meaning and power of dreams and visions as they are detailed in the Word of God. They are as much a part of the promise of the Father as is unknown tongues.

Fighting the Good Fight
By Ronald W. Crawford

We are at war! The key to victory is not found in our weapons, but in our attitudes. God will grant to us triumph as we grant to Him our perceptions.

Manual of Five-Fold Interpretation
By Ronald W. Crawford

God desires to communicate with His church today! One of the ways in which this specific word from God will be conveyed and interpreted is through these five comprehensive offices: apostle, prophet, teachers, evangelist and pastor.

Proskuneo
By Ronald W. Crawford

The posture of prayer for the time in which we live is clearly stated within the Word of the Lord. The Bible clearly tells us that in heaven and on earth we must lay all that we are before Him in prayer.

Right Hand and Left Hand
By Ronald W. Crawford

A collection of sermons concerning the right and left in scripture. God has much to say regarding this vital insight, and He intends for you to know it. A grasp of the essential truth of relationship and acquisition could mean the difference between blessing and defeat in your life.

Selah
By Ronald W. Crawford

Throughout the writings of David, the concept of Selah is mentioned over seventy times. This powerful word indicates much more than a pause for reflection. Selah is that juncture that connects the promises of God with their fulfillment. Selah is the manner in which God causes His children to step into their heritage of blessing and power. We must understand and embrace the Selah if we are to move within the Tabernacle of David.

Seven Thunders Revealed
By Ronald W. Crawford

The Word of God tells us exactly how His children are to move within the authority of His heavenly Throne. A very clear progression of four stages of power is depicted within the Book of Revelation. God will use this mighty principle of righteous rule to change the planet. This understanding is a must for anyone that desires to be used of God in these last days..

Sprinkling of the Blood
By Ronald W. Crawford

The Blood of Christ is essential in the process of salvation, but our need for the blood does not end at the inception of the Christian life. There is a blood sprinkling that is readily declared in the New Covenant, and we must utilize this sprinkling in order to move progressively forward into the deeper things of God.

Stork Women of Shinar
By Ronald W. Crawford

What is located in the place of ancient Babylon? What is the identity of the feminine spirits that have taken the ephah of wickedness to this ancient place? How do we overcome them for the cause of righteousness?

The Timing of God
By Ronald W. Crawford

Timing is vital in all that we do, whether in the natural or spiritual realm. When we grasp the importance of the timing of God, we will position ourselves for miracles.

His Kingdom Come
By Paul David Harrison

The missing element of the gospel message is as Jesus prayed, "His kingdom come." This study presents how absolutely essential it is to preach about the kingdom of God including the Biblical precedent for preaching about angels and the things of the spiritual realm.

SAINTS' NETWORK AUTHORS

Breaking Chains of Darkness
By Charles Baker, PhD.

The author explains the tactics of the enemy in establishing strongholds in Christians and how they can be ended by the power of the Blood of Jesus.

School of the Saints   By Mark Burke

Many Christians have been drinking milk too long. God is releasing fresh manna and meat from heaven, opening the eyes of understanding and training His saints for these last days. Will you enroll in God's school of the saints?

Training of a Saint   By Mark Burke

We must ask the Father to open our spirits to receive the deep truths of His kingdom. We need the anointings of God to understand and comprehend all that He is currently saying to His church. We must be trained to be people who grasp what the Lord is doing, the saints.

Preparing His Own   By Dennis Stewart

This three-volume series is a practical review of Jesus' teachings to His twelve disciples during the beginning, middle and end of His ministry. The simple premise is to discover all you can about what Jesus wanted His disciples to know and in the process you will discover what Jesus wants you to know.

The City Taking Anointing   By David Wright

Covenant is the basis of our Lord's redemptive process. It is time for you to understand and appropriate powerful covenant principles such as the creational covenant of worship and the everlasting covenant, to transform your city into the place of its destiny in the coming glory of the Lord.

PNEUMATIKOS PUBLISHING

P.O. Box 595351, Dallas, Texas 75359
(214) 821-5290 fax (214) 821-0670
www.pneumatikos.com or email info@pneumatikos.com

about the author

Pastor Ron Crawford was raised in Pittsburgh, Pennsylvania, where he faithfully attended a Pentecostal church with his family. He gave his life to the Lord at a very young age and received the baptism in the Holy Spirit with the evidence of speaking in other tongues as a young teenager. He was called into the ministry and pursued a BA in Bible at Central Bible College, followed by a master's degree in Biblical Studies at the Assemblies of God Theological Seminary. During his college years he met and married his lovely wife, Debbie, and they have two daughters, Kelly and Katy. Upon graduation, Pastor Crawford accepted an invitation to join the staff at Lakewood Assembly of God in Dallas, Texas. After serving on staff for seven years, he was elected Senior Pastor in 1987, where he still pastors today.

PERILAMPO
(water color art by Isai Hernandez)

And there were in the same country shepherds abiding in the field, keeping watch over their flock by night. [9]And, lo, the angel of the Lord came upon them, and the glory of the Lord shone round about them: and they were sore afraid. [10]And the angel said unto them, Fear not: for, behold, I bring you good tidings of great joy, which shall be to all people. [11]For unto you is born this day in the city of David a Saviour, which is Christ the Lord. [12]And this *shall be* a sign unto you; Ye shall find the babe wrapped in swaddling clothes, lying in a manger. [13]And suddenly there was with the angel a multitude of the heavenly host praising God, and saying, [14]Glory to God in the highest, and on earth peace, good will toward men. [15]And it came to pass, as the angels were gone away from them into heaven, the shepherds said one to another, Let us now go even unto Bethlehem, and see this thing which is come to pass, which the Lord hath made known unto us. [16]And they came with haste, and found Mary, and Joseph, and the babe lying in a manger. [17]And when they had seen *it,* they made known abroad the saying which was told them concerning this child. [18]And all they that heard *it* wondered at those things which were told them by the shepherds. [19]But Mary kept all these things, and pondered *them* in her heart. [20]And the shepherds returned, glorifying and praising God for all the things that they had heard and seen, as it was told unto   them.

Luke 2:8-20